the perfect bag

Linda McGehee

©2006 Linda McGehee
Published by

krause publications
An Imprint of F+W Publications

700 East State Street • Iola, WI 54990-0001
715-445-2214 • 888-457-2873

Our toll-free number to place an order or obtain
a free catalog is (800) 258-0929.

Library of Congress Catalog Number: 2006934235

ISBN 13-digit: 978-0-89689-409-9
ISBN 10-digit: 0-89689-409-6

Designed by Heidi Bittner-Zastrow
Edited by Erica Swanson and Susan Sliwicki
Photography by Jack A. Williams and Krause Publications

Printed in the United States of America

acknowledgments

Nothing worthwhile is accomplished without the support of others —
a thread is nothing without a needle and fabric. A needle needs motivation and direction.
I need a sewing machine. It's the ongoing process of collection and dependency on others
that has allowed me to create this book. I wish to thank those who have been involved with
my venture by supplying inspiration, products and equipment.

Of course my parents, my sister and my two brothers who helped me set my goals.

I acknowledge the encouragement and sewing expertise from my Aunts Toto and Lois.

My utmost appreciation goes to my students and customers, who have kept me motivated through the years.

A very special thank you goes to my colleagues in the industry who have enlightened me with questions and answers.

Thank you to the individuals who entered Ghee's Handbag Challenge.

Thank you to the following companies that provided:

Sewing machine and accessories:
Baby Lock USA, Bernina of America, Inc., Brother International, Elna USA, Husqvarna Viking, Janome New Home, PFAFF American Sales Corp. and Singer.

Batting, Fusibles, & Interfacing:
Staple Aids Sewing Corp. and The Warm Company.

Buttons: Designs by Dawn, and It's a Button

Cutting Equipment: OLFA

Fabrics:
Benartex, Inc., Fabric-Quilt, Inc., Hoffman California Fabrics, Loralie and Toray Ultrasuede (America), Inc.

Handbag Hardware: Ghee's

Threads:
Coats & Clark, Inc., Gutermann of America, Inc., Kreinik Mfg. Co. Inc. Mettler Threads, OESD, Sulky of America, Superior Threads and YLI Corp.

Needles: Schmetz

I am most grateful to Nancy, my main support system at Ghee's, who has been with me probably longer than she cares to admit.

My special thanks to Susan, Erica and Heidi at Krause Publication for making my ideas look wonderful in book form.

Words cannot express how grateful I am to my life partner, my husband, Jack, who has stood by me through hills and valleys, and who has helped me make my life what it is today. It was his idea to start the "little business." Jack's expertise with the camera, originally 35mm and now digital, has bonded us to make this book truly a partnership of sewing and photography.

My thanks to each of you for helping to make my life fun while enabling me to follow my dreams.

table of contents

Introduction

EACH HANDBAG IS AN ADVENTURE — I have an idea when I begin, but I really don't know how the bag will turn out. When I design a pattern for a new bag, one of my primary concerns is to incorporate new techniques. I love discovering simpler and better ways to add a zipper or a pocket, and incorporating technology and time-tested classic sewing skills to create brand-new methods. As I learn to use the tools and technology available nowadays, I want to pass my "tricks" on to other sewers. Hopefully they will spark creativity — and they may even be an inspiration to sew more!

The Perfect Bag is oblong-shaped and has many useful pockets to make it suitable for day or evening, fancy or sport. The shape of the pattern pieces makes it easy to construct the bag using a larger opening at the top and a smaller base, or a smaller opening at the top and a larger base. The multi-size pattern will allow you to create a bag to carry small items or a multitude of accessories. A small bag is 8" x 10", medium is 10" x 12", large is 12" x 15" and large with gusset is 14" x 17". Close the lined handbag with a magnetic snap or a button with a loop.

A zipped "secret" pocket is stitched into the lining seam allowance. The large size includes an optional gusset with its own style of secret pocket. A variety of pocket options for cell phones, keys, glasses and other handy items makes your stylish bag practical. Choose the pockets that make the bag perfect for you.

I am guided by two objectives: I always want my bags to be functional and stylish. So, as you begin to make your own bag, consider the possibilities. Choose the size you like; begin with a fun and stylish fabric; include pockets to organize your belongings; and add embellishments to suit your taste. Create The Perfect Bag.

Definitions

Every specialized activity develops a unique vocabulary.
The following glossary of words and phrases used in this book will allow you to
create your custom designs and avoid misunderstanding.

Appliqué:

A design applied to the surface of another fabric using hand or machine stitching, glue or bonding; to apply designs to the surface of another fabric.

Batting:

A thin or fluffy layer of natural or synthetic non-woven fibers used between layers of fabric to give soft support for quilting.

Bias:

A diagonal line other than the lengthwise or cross-grain of fabric. True bias makes a 45-degree angle across the lengthwise and cross-grain. It ravels less and has greater stretch and give than any other cut edge.

Bobbin Thread:

Thread designed to use specifically in the bobbin when decorative thread is used in the needle. This thread is lightweight, and it is not designed for bag construction.

Bond:

To make into one, as in bonding fabric to fleece using a thin layer of fusible medium.

Butt:

To push together so the edges meet and just touch rather than overlap. Use this technique to construct a strap of heavy fabric.

Continuous Bias:

Continuing without a break; an unbroken or uncut strip of fabric cut on the diagonal or bias grain of the fabric.

Corded Piping:

A narrow fold of fabric filled with cord — used for trimming seams to add dimension and definition.

Couching:

A method of stitching in which you build a design by hand or machine stitching over threads, cords, braids or yarns laid on fabric.

Cross-grain:

The weft, threads or yarns running across a fabric from selvage to selvage.

Cutting Mat:

The cutting surface used with a rotary cutter to avoid marring the table and damaging the cutting blade.

D-Ring:

A metal or plastic ring in the shape of the letter D — used to make an adjustable strap.

Fashion Fabric:

Fabric visible on the finished project. It is not necessarily the side of the fabric designed to be the right side. Sometimes the wrong side is more pleasing to the eye or adds better contrast.

Feet:

Metal or plastic added to the bottom of a bag to keep it from getting dirty.

Fleece:

Any of the various soft or woolly battings or needle punch used for underlining — not to be confused with Polarfleece.

Fusible Web:

The resin coating on the back of interfacing used to bond to fabric with the application of heat and moisture; a web-like material that melts when heat is applied. Refer to the manufacturer's instructions to use.

Fusible Fleece:

Fleece or needle punch, with a thin layer of fusible medium applied to one side, which makes it easier to bond fabric to the fleece. Using fusible fleece means that you don't have to use fleece and a fusible medium when bonding layers together.

Fussy Cut:

To cut a specific portion from a fabric for a particular detail or interest.

Grain:

The warp or lengthwise threads or yarns of a fabric parallel to the selvage.

Interfacing:

The fabric placed on the lining or inside of a handbag to give body, strength and support. Interfacing is fusible or sew-in; knitted, woven or non-woven; and made of natural or synthetic fibers.

Leftovers:

Remaining fabric after project is complete. Leftovers are not junk, waste or trash — they are creative opportunities. Use leftovers for lagniappe (a little something extra) projects once the first project is finished.

Need:

Something useful, required, or desired that is lacking; state of extreme want as in fabric, thread, sewing equipment. Sometimes you need to indulge yourself.

Needle Position:

On most machines, can be moved left or right of the center.

Magnetic Snap:

The catch used at the opening of a handbag for magnetic closure. Prongs on the backside attach it to the bag.

Needle Punch:

A dense, non-woven sheet of polyester punched with thousands of polyester fibers; it is sold by the yard for stuffing or stabilizing heavier projects.

Pin Tuck:

A small, flat fold stitched in a garment for ornamental or utility purposes. The stitch produces tuck effects as a twin needle sews a fold in the fabric.

Piping:

A narrow fold of fabric that trims seams to add dimension and definition.

Pivot:

To turn the fabric with the needle inserted to hold a position.

Presser Foot:

The portion of the sewing machine that guards the needle and rests on the feed dogs, causing the machine to feed the fabric. There is a wide variety of presser feet available for various types of sewing.

Rip:

To remove unwanted stitches. As ye sew, so shall ye rip.

Rotary Cutter:

A fabric-cutting device with an extremely sharp, round blade — looks like a pizza wheel.

Sew-in Magnetic Snap:

The magnetic catch used to close the opening of a handbag. It has holes to attach it to the bag with hand or machine stitches.

Shoulder Pad:

An oval-shaped piece, usually plastic or fabric, which a strap slides through to balance the weight of the bag on the shoulder.

Slide:

The portion of a zipper that opens and closes the teeth.

Slider:

A metal or plastic part that makes a handbag strap adjustable.

Swivel Snap:

A clasp or fastener, much like the clip on a dog leash, used to make detachable or adjustable straps. You can use it with a short strap attached to the inside of a bag to hold a key ring.

Choosing Ingredients

Select from a wide range of materials to customize your bag.
Fabric could be your starting point — but don't forget about zippers, buttons and
all of the little extras that add up to a totally unique handbag.

Magnetic Snap or Button:

You will need something to close the bag. A decorative button with a loop could hold the bag closed — and add to the overall design. Conversely, the button could detract from the embellishment on the bag. A magnetic snap, whether sew-in or applied with prongs, is perfect to hold the bag closed.

Fashion Fabric:

Most fabrics are suitable for handbags. The under construction will vary, depending on the weight of the fabric. You can use cotton, quilting weight fabrics, silk Dupioni, brocade, denim, tapestry and other home decoration fabrics, like faux suede, ticking and leather.

Fleece:

The weight of fleece used for support in the bag is determined by the weight of the fashion fabric and the size of the bag. Use heavyweight fleece on lightweight fashion fabric and lightweight fleece on heavy fashion fabric. Also, consider the size of the finished bag; use lightweight fleece on small bags and heavyweight fleece on large bags. Some heavier fabrics, like tapestry, don't need extra support.

tip:

You can avoid making a big mess with the iron during the fusing process by choosing fusible fleece. Because the fusible fleece is one unit, you can't accidentally cut the fusible web larger than the fleece.

Make sure the fusing portion is facing the wrong side of the fabric rather than the iron. If you do get fusible web on the iron, use dryer sheets to clean it immediately. When the fusible web is baked on the iron, use an iron cleaner to remove the buildup.

tip:

To save time, fuse the fleece to the fashion fabric before cutting.

Different companies manufacture different weights of fleece. When in doubt, test by fusing a small piece of fleece to the fabric.

A large bag made of heavy fabric may require support, but you could end up with bulky seam allowances. Remove the seam allowance of the fleece before fusing to the fashion fabric to eliminate bulk.

Fusible Web:

A wide range of fusible web in various weights is available. Some paper-backed webs come with specific instructions for appliqué or crafts. They may be purchased by the yard or in a small package. Generally, the best choice for a handbag is a lightweight fusible web without paper backing. I prefer to avoid a cutting step by using fusible fleece rather than fleece and fusible web.

tip:

To save time and avoid a cutting step, fuse interfacing to the lining before cutting. It will stabilize the lining, keep soft lining fabrics from slipping and shrink the interfacing and assure that the pieces match perfectly.

Lining:

Fabric used for the lining should complement the bag and carry the design from the outside to the inside — so always use pretty lining rather than leftover scraps.

Fusible Interfacing:

To add support to the lining and prevent it from raveling, use fusible interfacing. I prefer the knit-type interfacing because it gives the proper weight and flow to the lining. It does not leave little bumps on the right side of the fabric or make the weight feel like cardboard.

Zippers:

They may be functional or decorative, or both. Zippers used in a handbag should be sturdy enough to handle wear and tear. Zippers with decorative teeth, heavier sport zippers and rhinestone zippers are both fashionable and functional. The zipper used for the secret pocket or lining pockets does not need to be decorative.

Corded Piping:

To define the different sections of the handbag and give shape to the curves of the bag, use corded piping. Decorative corded piping is available by the yard. Choose the size that is appropriate for your bag's style and size. You can also make your own corded piping using a companion or contrasting fabric.

Yardages and Notions

This pattern has multiple design opportunities. The yardage for each size includes several pockets. It is okay to add more or use fewer pockets — this is your own personal choice. The yardages for pattern pieces are shown on the cutting layouts. Any changes may alter the amount of fabric necessary for the bag.

Yardage and Notions
for Fashion Fabric and Lining

Small	Medium	Large	Large with Gusset	
1	1	1	1 or 2	**Magnetic Snap or Button**
½ yd.	¾ yd.	1¼ yd.	1¼ yd.	**Fashion Fabric (45")**
½ yd.	¾ yd.	1¼ yd.	1¼ yd.	**Fleece (45")**
½ yd.	¾ yd.	1¼ yd.	1¼ yd.	**Fusible Web (60")***
½ yd.	⅝ yd.	⅞ yd.	1 yd.	**Lining (45")**
½ yd.	⅝ yd.	⅞ yd.	1 yd.	**Fusible Interfacing (60")**
2 yd.	2⅜ yd.	2¾ yd.	4¾ yd.	**Corded Piping**
12"	12"	12"	12"	**Zipper**

Thread

*When using fusible fleece, it is not necessary to use fusible web.

Yardage and Notions
for Double-Faced Quilted Fabric

Small	Medium	Large	Large with Gusset	
1	1	1	1 or 2	Magnetic Snap or Button
½ yd.	¾ yd.	1¼ yd.	1¼ yd.	Double-faced Quilted Fabric (45")
½ yd.	½ yd.	1¼ yd.	1¼ yd.	Companion Fabric (45")
2 yd.	2⅜ yd.	2¾ yd.	4¾ yd.	Corded Piping
12"	12"	12"	12"	Zipper

Thread

Shopping Tips:

You may need additional fabric to match plaids, one-way designs and fussy cuts. Take pattern pieces or measurements along on a shopping trip when you will be using a combination of fabrics for the bag. Sometimes the corded piping and straps will be made of one fabric; other times the center panel will be one fabric and the sides and strap will be another.

It is better to have too much fabric than not enough, so don't cut yourself short when purchasing fabric. Who knows when you will want to make another creative venture — or when the scissors or rotary cutter will cut a little too far!

If you don't have quite enough fabric, get creative.

Use leftover fabric from garments to create a bag that matches an outfit. Complement the fabric with purchased corded piping or decorative handles. Leftover fabric is also perfect for making a matching wallet, eyeglass case or coin purse. You might even have enough scraps to make a small bag for a child to match Mom's.

Purchase fleece, fusible web and interfacing in larger quantities than you need to complete the pattern. These products are necessary for many different projects, so keep them on hand for spur-of-the-moment plans.

Zipper Tips:

The zipper listed in Yardage and Notions is designed for the secret pocket. Additional zippers may be desired for other pockets on the inside or outside of the bag.

Always purchase zippers that are longer than the desired length. It's easy to reduce the size of a zipper, but it's difficult to redesign when a zipper is too short.

Design Tips:

— A zipper, button or small embroidery sample can be the focal point of a bag

— Leftover piecing or quilt blocks make wonderful bags.

— When using leftover fabric to make a matching bag for an ensemble, make sure the bag does not blend into the outfit. Add decorative stitching, embroidery or appliqué for contrast. Too much of a good thing can make a boring outfit.

Cutting Layouts

These cutting layouts will help you cut the appropriate pieces for each bag. The basic pieces in the pattern are necessary; some other pieces are optional. Study the pieces, and choose the correct ones for the style of bag you want to make. There are lots of possibilities!

For fashion fabric, use #1, #2 and #4. For lining, use #4, #5 and #6. Choose #3 for a Strap, #10 to attach a Chain or #14 to attach a Decorative Handle. Optional Pockets are #7, #8, #9 and #13. Use #11 or #12 for the piecing option or as a flap.

Pattern Pieces:

#1 Fashion Fabric Center Panel

#2 Fashion Fabric Side Panel

#3 Strap

#4 Gusset

#5 Lining Center Panel

#6 Lining Side Panel

#7 Secret Pocket for Small, Medium, and Large

#8 Secret Pocket for Large with Gusset

#9 Pleated Patch Pocket for Lining

#10 Button Loop and Chain Loop

#11 Triangle for Piecing Option — Top

#12 Triangle for Piecing Option — Bottom

#13 Pleated Outside Pocket

#14 Handle Loop

Fashion Fabric Layout — Large with Gusset
Fleece, Fusible Web

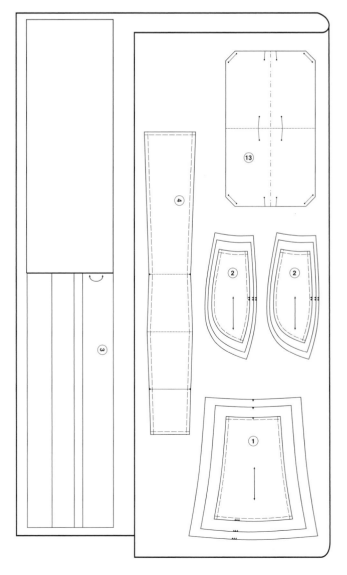

Lining Layout — Large with Gusset
Fusible Interfacing

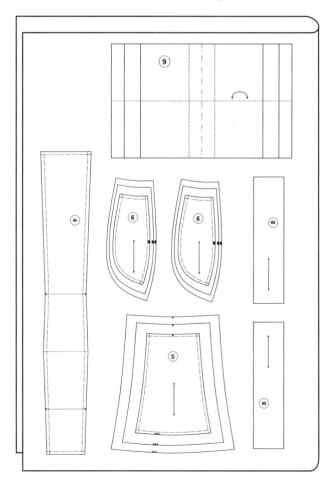

Fashion Fabric Layout — Large
Fleece, Fusible Web

Lining Layout — Large
Fusible Lining

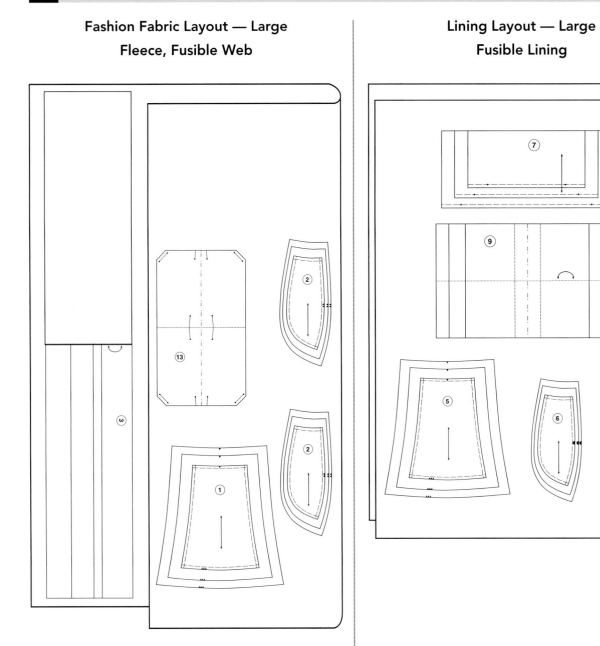

Fashion Fabric Layout — Medium

Lining Layout — Medium

Fashion Fabric Layout — Small

Lining Layout — Small

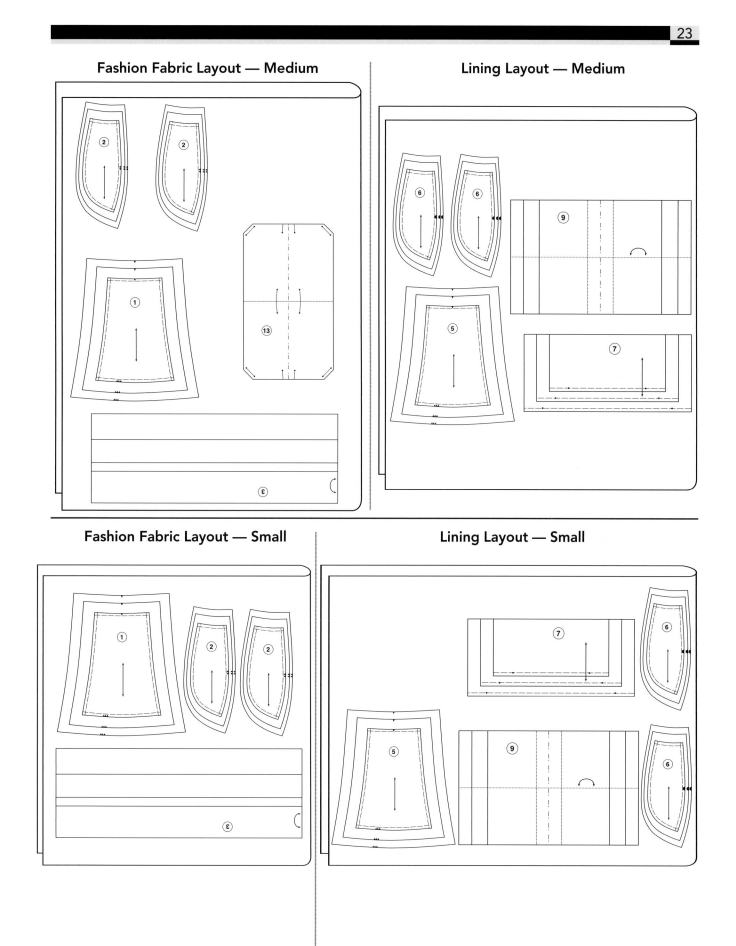

Basic Construction

Following simple instructions, you can begin to make a beautiful bag.
Choose the small, medium or large size, cut the right pieces, and start stitching!

fashion fabric

Use ¼" seam allowances to construct the bag unless otherwise noted. Using another seam allowance may keep the pieces from fitting together properly. This is a handbag pattern rather than a garment pattern — fitting a bag is not as crucial as fitting a garment, but it always makes me happy when the puzzle pieces fit together.

tip:

Most machines offer an optional ¼" quilting foot. Align the edge of the foot with the cut edge of the fabric for a perfect ¼" seam allowance. You may also use the all-purpose foot with the needle moved to the right, so the distance between the needle and the edge of the foot equals ¼".

Place pins perpendicular (at a right angle) to the seam, and it will be easy to pull the pins out as the foot reaches them. If you place the pins parallel to the seam, the heads will invariably be pointing the wrong direction.

Careful! It is not a good idea to stitch over pins. Should the needle come in contact with the pin, the needle will be burred and cause pull lines on the fabric. It could also break the needle.

Because you will be stitching on bulky fabric, use a large needle. Depending on the fabric, a 90/14 or 100/16 needle is appropriate. Sometimes a jeans needle works best. If your needle is breaking frequently, it is probably too small.

Place fusible web (#1 and #2) between wrong side of fashion fabric (#1 and #2) and fleece (#1 and #2). Follow the manufacturer's instructions to bond the layers. Generally, you must use the wool setting on a steam iron. The weight and type of fabric will determine the amount of steam. There may be a button to regulate the amount of steam — in that case, use the maximum setting. Other irons have a button to produce a shot of steam. Sometimes you have to do both for perfect bonding.

tip:

Some manufacturers require you to use steam, while others recommend that you use dry heat during the bonding process. Be sure to follow the instructions for the product that you purchase.

If necessary, use a wet press cloth to bond properly.

Know your iron and its peculiarities. To steam properly, the iron should be set at the wool setting. When the heat is set too low, the iron will water spot rather than steam. If the iron is set too high, the iron may scorch the fabric, fleece, or interfacing. Test on a scrap to avoid a catastrophe.

Some manufacturers include a plastic liner with instructions on the bolt of their products. Often people throw away these instructions. To keep the important information handy, use two sets of instructions and make a plastic bag to hold leftover fleece or interfacing. Simply fold the instructions in half lengthwise or crosswise, depending on the liner, and baste the outside edges together. One side of instructions may be upside down — that's okay. Using two or more sets of instructions will create a bag large enough to hold the leftovers and have full instructions on one side of the bag without having to flip it over. This bag has several purposes: It keeps the interfacing tidy, organizes the instructions and makes inventory quick and easy.

Use your imagination to decorate the bag, or refer to the Embellishing with Threads or Strip Piecing Option chapters for inspiration. See the Outside Pockets chapter if you want pockets on the outside of the bag.

Sometimes design elements change as the style of the bag changes. Originally, the single notch was designed as the top of the bag, and the triple notch was designed as the bottom. This created a bag with a wider bottom and narrow top. But using the single notch as the bottom and the triple notch as the top created an entirely different bag. Which style should you choose? It's up to you!

The bag's decorative element may help determine which design is appropriate. One style, with the wider opening, lends itself to a double strap or handle, while the narrow opening calls for a longer, single strap. There is no right or wrong answer, but it is important to be consistent. Whatever edge is chosen as the top edge of the fashion fabric should also be used with the corresponding lining piece (#5).

begin sewing

Place right sides of fashion fabric center panels (#1) together, matching notches. Stitch the triple-notched edge using a ¼" seam allowance. Press seam allowance open.

tip:

There are many opportunities with this versatile pattern! The center panel fits to the side panels, with the triple notch as the top or bottom. Notice that the center panel has equal-length sides.

tip:

Sometimes a ¼" seam allowance will refuse to stay open. Use the edge-stitching or joining foot to edge stitch the seam allowance and keep it permanently flat. On the right side of the fabric, with the bar of the foot in the center of the seam allowance, move the needle to the left or right several notches. The needle position should be about ¹⁄₁₆" (but no more than ⅛") from the seam allowance. Begin stitching to hold the seam allowance flat. Stitch each side of the seam allowance in the same manner to form edge stitching, so that the seam allowance is flat and maintains the proper curve.

Notice the difference in the side panel that was not edge stitched.

attaching corded piping

1 Align the cut edge of the piping along the two long cut edges of #1, making sure the bottom seam allowance stays pressed open. Place corded piping under the pearls or piping foot. Move needle away from cord by changing needle position one notch from the position closest to corded piping.

tips:

• *For accuracy, use the pearl & piping foot rather than the zipper foot. The groove in the foot keeps the stitching the perfect distance from the cord, rather than too close or too far away.*

• *Use a longer stitch length to keep from stretching the corded piping.*

2 Stitch in place using a slightly larger stitch length. Refer to the Finishing Detail chapter for more involved instructions and ideas.

3 Place right sides of fashion fabric (#2) side panels together, matching notches. Stitch along the double-notched edge.

4 With right sides together, match seam allowances previously stitched, and stitch the center panel (#1) to the side panels (#2). Use the stitching line that attaches the corded piping as a guide. Move needle position closer to the corded piping to keep previous stitching from showing on the right side. Ease the curved edge around the side panel to fit the straight area of the center panel.

tip:

Whenever possible, use the clothesline approach to stitch seams — continue stitching another seam allowance without breaking the stitches. This method saves thread and keeps you from having to trim too many threads from each end of the seam allowance.

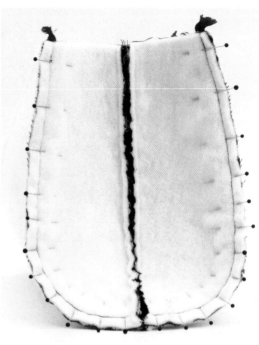

5 Eventually, the opening edge is stitched to the lining. To remove extra bulk from the corded piping in the seam allowance area, pull the cord and trim it away to the seam line. After trimming, run your finger over the corded piping to relax the cord.

6 Since there is no seam allowance to hide the beginning or ending of the corded piping, use continuous corded piping at the opening edge to finish the upper portion of the bag connected to the lining. Choose an inconspicuous place to begin, like the side seam of the bag. Leave a 1" tail at the beginning. Pull 1" of cording from the piping and cut it off. Place cut edge of corded piping even with opening edge of bag. Stitch around the opening of the bag with the side seam allowances open and the center panel seam allowances facing toward the side panels.

tip:

The corded piping of the side seams should face the center of the bag.

7 Continue stitching the corded piping to the opening, and return to the beginning with the 1" tail. Curve the original 1" tail toward the outside edge of the bag. Pull and trim the cord from the stitched piping, so the trimmed cord at the beginning of this row of stitching barely touches the trimmed cord at the end of the row. Overlap the piping slightly, and curve toward the cut edge. Once the lining is stitched to the bag, there will be a smooth finish to the corded piping.

lining construction

To add pockets to the lining, refer to the Inside Pockets chapter.

tip:

To save time and eliminate a cutting step, fuse the interfacing to the lining before cutting.

1 Place front and back Lining Center Panel (#5) pieces together, and stitch bottom seam allowance. Make sure the corresponding seam is stitched on the fashion fabric.

2 Place lining fabric of Lining Side Panels (#6) right sides together, matching notches. Stitch along the notched edge. Attach lining side panels to lining center panel in the same manner as the fashion fabric, but leave out the corded piping.

tip:

The secret pocket has an opening for turning. If you decide to omit that pocket, leave an opening in the bottom of the lining to turn the bag later.

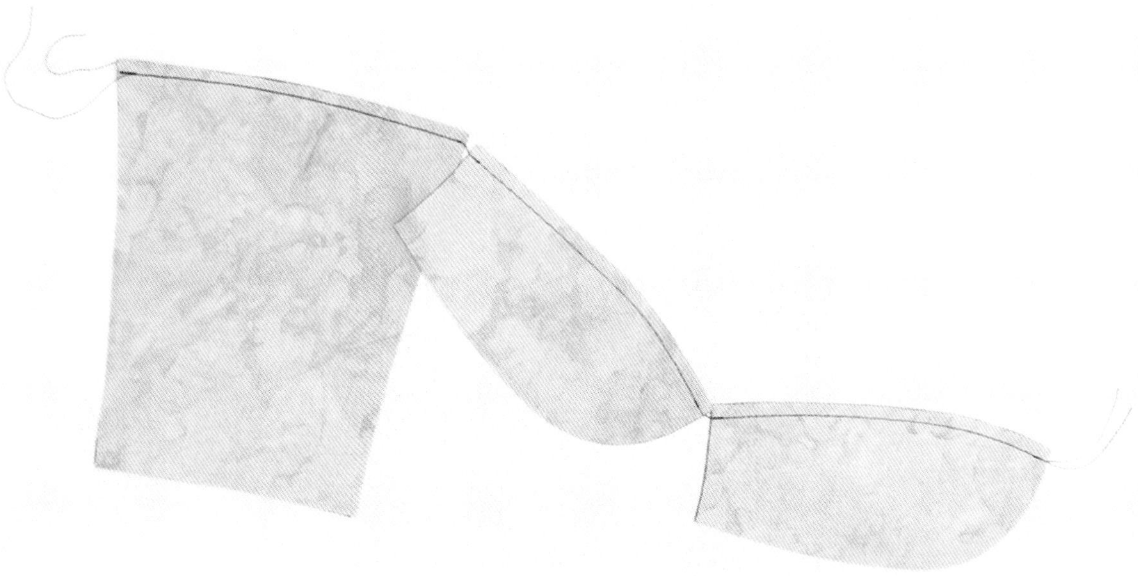

making a strap

There are many ways to make a strap or handle for the bag. Refer to the Straps and Handles chapter for more options.

1 Fold Strap (#3) in half lengthwise with wrong sides together. Press the length of the strap. Open the strap, and fold the cut edges to almost meet the center fold. Fold the strap in half lengthwise again to form four layers. Edge stitch both sides of the strap.

tip:

• *Allow about ⅛" of space between the lengthwise cut edges of the strap to eliminate bulk in the final folding. Turning the fabric causes the cut edges to press closer together, and this tiny bit of space prevents the cut layers from overlapping.*

• *Use additional stitching on the strap for decoration and durability.*

2 Attach the strap to the handbag on top of the side panel seam allowance, with the strap extending into open air about ½".

tip:

It is very easy for the strap to move as it is stitched to the side panel. To keep it from slipping, place the needle in the center of the strap, back tack and then stitch forward. The strap will stay in the proper position every time.

Be sure to use a ½" seam allowance on the ends of the strap for security and built-in grading.

attaching the lining

With right sides together (one inside the other), stitch upper edge of handbag to upper edge of lining. Turn right side out through the opening in the bottom.

applying snaps

You can choose from several sizes and types of magnetic snaps to close the bag. This is the basic snap application — other options are shown in the Finishing Detail chapter. Position the prongs of the snap on the right side of the lining, about ¾" from the center upper edge. Push the prongs through the lining. You may need to clip small slits to avoid ripping the fabric. Place the metal support piece over the prongs on the wrong side of the lining. Use pliers to bend the prongs flat. Slipstitch or edge stitch an opening in the bottom of the pocket lining.

tip:

Use a thin laminated cardboard or plastic template to make a support disk to protect the lining fabric from being cut by the metal disk. I like to use an empty soda container.

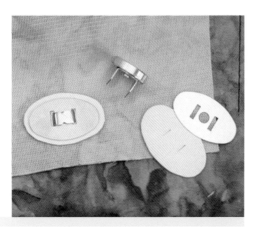

instructions for large bag with gusset

1 Stitch the seam allowance along the stitching line at the center bottom of the gusset.

tip:

For an added design feature, apply contrasting binding to the top edge of the pockets. You can also top stitch the foldline on the pocket.

2 To form the pocket in each end of the gusset, bring the dotted notched foldline to match the solid notched line. Baste the triple layer of seam allowances to hold the pockets in place.

3 Attach corded piping to the long sides of the gusset.

4 Create pockets as desired for the center panel.

tip:

Gently pull the cord from the piping, being careful not to pull too much. If you pull the cord too far, you can't replace it without ripping the piping and starting over.

5 Attach corded piping on each side of the center panel, leaving a 1" tail on each end. Remove the excess cord from the piping to the crossing seam line of the opening. This amount should be approximately 1¼".

6 Pin and stitch a side panel to each side of the center panel. Ease along the curved edge to fit the straight edge.

7 Match the bottom seam of the gusset to the center bottom of the bag, and insert the gusset between the front center panel/side panel section and back center panel/side section to form the bag. Construct the lining like you did the fashion fabric, using pockets as desired. Be sure to leave an opening for turning. Attach the strap to each end of the gusset. Apply corded piping to the opening edge. With right sides together, one inside the other, stitch the opening edge of the bag to the lining. Attach the snap to close. Slipstitch or edge stitch the opening in the lining.

optional binding at opening

You can bind the opening edge instead of placing right sides together, stitching and turning through a hole. It is easiest to bind the small bag with the narrow bottom and wide opening edge. After completing the lining and outside fabric, place the wrong sides together, with the lining inside the bag. Insert the magnetic snap. Baste the edges together. Trim excess piping and other decoration.

Attach the binding to the opening edge, beginning at the side seam. Finish the bag with straps.

Inside Pockets

Make organization easy and convenient with pockets for essentials. Find out what you need to carry, and make the appropriate pockets to suit your needs. Accessible pockets for pens, lipstick, business cards, receipts, cell phone, iPod, notepad, maps and other essentials keep items ready to use, but are not cumbersome.

pleated patch pockets

Constructing the durable pleated patch pocket for the lining is quick and easy. Use pattern piece #9. Following the pattern layout, cut this piece from lining and interfacing. Always interface the fabric before cutting to save a cutting step. This also reinforces light-weight fabrics like silk. You don't have to match the lining fabric to the pocket — variety is the spice of life.

1 Fold the lining, wrong sides together, following the first foldline on the pattern. This will add more support to the pocket.

2 Match the two foldlines to the center to create a pleat. Follow the instructions to complete the pleated pocket in the Using Double-Faced Quilting Fabric chapter.

tip:

You don't have to place the pleat in the center of the bag. You can customize the size of the pockets by shifting the pleat.

secret pocket in bottom seam

1 To insert the secret pocket, place right side of the Lining Center Panel (#5) to right side of zipper, with the zipper extending from both ends of the lining. Sandwich the zipper between the lining and Secret Pocket (#7), with the right side of the pocket next to the wrong side of the zipper.

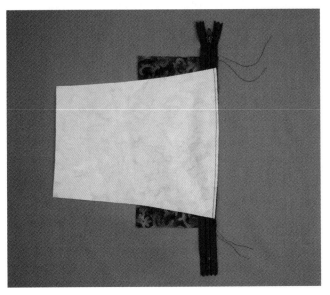

2 Align the all-purpose foot next to the edge of the zipper, and move the needle position as close to the zipper coil as possible. Stitch the length of the zipper.

tip: *You won't be able to see the zipper while you are stitching. The presser foot should feel the zipper coil through the layer of lining fabric and ride against it rather than on top of it.*

There is no need to back tack when stitching, since another row of stitching will secure this seam, too.

3 Pull the pocket away from the zipper, with the lining facing the opposite direction. Edge stitch to hold flat.

4 Roll the lining close to the zipper and edge stitch.

Back side of zipper, with two rows of stitching.

5 Repeat the same process on other side of the zipper, aligning edges of lining and pocket right sides together.

Back side of pocket

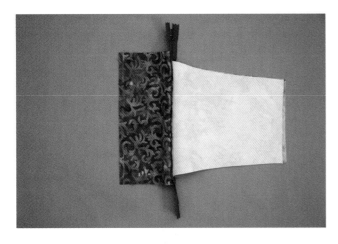

6 Match bottom edges of pocket pieces and stitch seam, leaving an opening shown by the dots to turn the bag later.

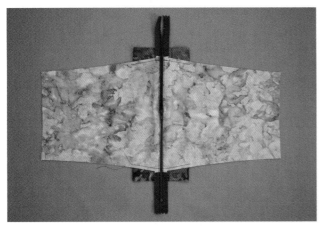

7 With zipper closed, fold pocket so that the opening for turning is underneath the zipper coil. There will be a tunnel under the zipper forming a pocket. The zipper becomes the bottom seam of the lining. Unzip the zipper halfway, and bar tack zipper on both ends. Machine baste along the seam allowances, using a scant ¼" seam to form the pocket.

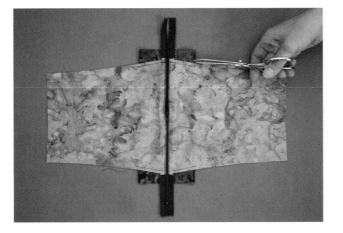

8 Trim excess pocket and zipper tape.

9 Be certain the zipper is open so you don't accidentally cut off the slider. Continue making the bag as if there were no secret pocket.

tip:

Never cut a zipper until you are sure the slider is in the proper position. In other words, make certain that the zipper works before trimming the excess. Nothing is more aggravating than finding the zipper slider in the trash!

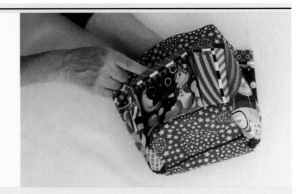

secret pocket in gusset

The secret pocket in the gusset differs slightly from the secret pocket in the double-faced quilted fabric.

1 Follow the steps for the original secret pocket, using two layers of lining fabric rather than the pocket and center panel piece.

2 Finish the ends with binding. Lay the pocket on top of the lining gusset, and continue to make the lining.

Outside Pockets

Stay neat and prepared with pockets. The perfect bag has the right amount of zipper pockets and open pockets. Use zipper pockets to protect essentials, and choose open pockets for easy access. Don't use too many — they can be frustrating unless you are extremely organized.

outside zipper pocket

There are many types of zippers, and choosing only one can be difficult. Let the zipper become the focal point of the bag — sometimes it determines which fabric to choose, and sometimes it enhances the fabric. These Riri zippers could stand alone as the embellishment.

To join two zippers together, the zipper coils must be the same type.

It is easier to make something larger and trim it down to the perfect size than to build up a too-small object. This is true in the case of a zipper pocket. There are too many variables with zippers to make a zipper pocket by beginning with the perfect pattern piece. The zipper tape or coil may be large for decoration or small for utility; more zipper tape may be exposed for design work on one project and barely show on another. So, begin with a piece of fabric that is slightly larger than the intended size pocket, and use the excess zipper tape to decorate another area of the bag.

Most jacket zippers are 22" or longer. This particular pocket is about ½" larger than the Fashion Fabric Center Panel (#1).

tip:

Sports zippers are sturdy enough for handbags, too. YKK has a variety of bright and pastel separating zippers. Choose two zippers in complementary colors, unzip them and swap the colors.

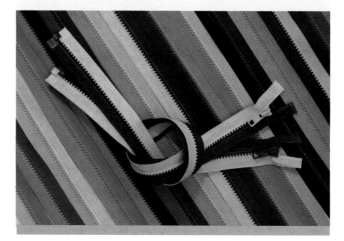

1 Using a rotary cutter, cut the pocket at the angle that best suits your needs. Sometimes the zipper opening may be perfectly horizontal, while other times it is more practical for the opening to be slightly angled from the upper portion of one side to the lower portion of the other side.

2 Align the cut edge of the fabric with the edge of the zipper. Using the all-purpose foot riding against the zipper, and the needle to the far left position, stitch the length of the zipper.

3 Fold the fabric over to expose the zipper coil. Position the edge-stitching foot with the bar between the zipper coil and the fold of the fabric. Move the needle position slightly left of the fold, and stitch across. Place the zipper pocket on another layer of center panel fabric, and trim to match.

tip:

On a small bag with an outside zipper pocket, place the zipper opening at a slight angle to make it easier to put things in the pocket.

pleated outside pocket

Basically, pleats are a series of folds in the fabric. There are two ways to construct pleated outside pockets — you can make a box pleat or an inverted pleat. A box pleat has two folds turned away from each other, with the folds underneath meeting at the center on the underside. Inverted pleats are box pleats in reverse — folds are turned toward each other and meet on the outside of the fabric.

pleated outside pocket in lightweight fabric

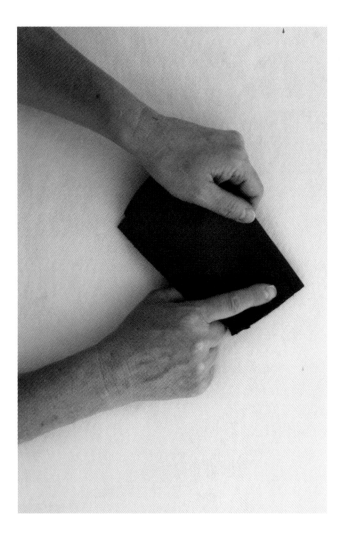

1 Place fusible web between the layers of folded pocket, and bond them together. Fold the pocket along the center line, mark the stitching line and stitch in place to form the pleat.

2 Choose either the box pleat or the inverted pleat. Stitch the center of the pleat to hold flat and secure.

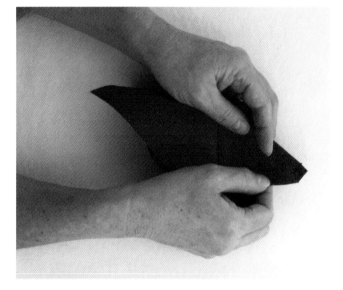

3 Fold the corner and stitch the angle.

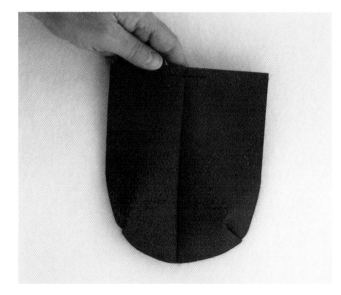

4 The corner stitching automatically forms a curve. Fold under ¼" around the outer edge of the pocket. Edge stitch the pocket to the center panel.

tips:

- *It is easier to place the fusible web on the fabric and bond the layers together before cutting than it is to cut the layers and bond them together later.*

- *If you use fusible web that does not have a paper backing, use a Teflon protective sheet to prevent dirtying the iron.*

- *Use a keyhole punch to remove the dots on the pattern. Transfer the dots onto the fabric with a fabric marker.*

- *To keep objects from falling to the bottom of the bag, be sure to attach patch pockets on the upper portion of the center panel.*

Thread Embellishing

There are infinite decorative work possibilities because of the numerous threads and built-in machine stitches available today. Some heavy threads are designed to stitch well in the machine needle; others are too heavy for the needle and should be used for couching.

heavy thread for the needle

Decorative stitching falls into two categories: threads for the needle and threads for the foot (or couching threads). There are many different heavy threads. Look for threads with color, shine or glitz that work easily in the needle of your machine. You can even use all sorts of combinations in one project. Experiment with variegated, rayon, polyester or metallic thread. For more variety, use jeans, quilting or topstitching thread.

Use a large eye needle, like a topstitching needle, to accommodate large, heavy threads, and use an all-purpose thread in the bobbin to balance its weight. Choose embroidery bobbin thread or pre-wound bobbins with metallic or shiny threads, like polyester or rayon.

Large, open stitches are practical for heavy threads. A long, straight stitch makes an effective design, too.

Straight lines stitched using a variegated quilting thread in a set stitch design pattern with the lines spaced ¼", ¾" and 1" apart. Stitch length is 3.5 to 4.

tip:

Do not use satin stitches with jeans or quilting threads. Save those stitches for metallic, rayon, polyester, fine cotton, silk or other fine threads. Experiment with stitches and thread on a scrap, and keep the tests as a reference. Note any alterations made to the stitching along with the stitch number. I like to keep a 3-ring binder for my testing samples.

Stitching lines can be straight and perfectly parallel in a pattern — or they can be undisciplined, randomly spaced and uneven.

Stitching with a double or triple needle makes an effective design.

Straight stitching in a wavy pattern randomly stitched to resemble a ribbon. Stitch length is 3.5 to 4.

couching thread

Couch one heavy thread or several heavy threads twisted together. You can also lay several heavy threads in a row and couch them to look like a ribbon, or work with ribbon floss — and these are just a few ideas to get you started! To make the techniques easier, there are sewing machine feet designed for each task. The more you experiment, the more you will discover your machine's thread, yarn, and ribbon capabilities.

Use the braiding or couching foot, which has a larger hole at the center to guide a small braid, heavier twisted threads, ribbon, yarn or cord — it will make couching a simple embellishment technique. The foot keeps the heavier threads in place while the needle thread attaches them to the fabric. Each machine company has a couching foot, and some machines have several. It is important for the hole in the foot to be as close as possible to the size of the thread. If you are addicted to couching like I am, it will be worth the investment to have each size.

1 Slide the couching thread through the hole in the foot, and attach it to the machine. Use a decorative embroidery thread in the needle. I prefer to use a variegated thread in the needle for color and sparkle as the couching thread is attached. Use the appropriate needle for the stitching thread. I prefer a topstitching needle, since I may shift from a shiny thread (rayon or polyester) to a metallic thread on the same project. Be sure to use lightweight bobbin thread. My favorite couching stitch is the multi-step zigzag stitch. Some machines call this an elastic stitch, and other machines have a similar darning stitch. Set the stitch length to 1.5 or 2.

2 Adjust to fit the width of the braid or twisted threads. Meander over the fabric according to your own artistic vision.

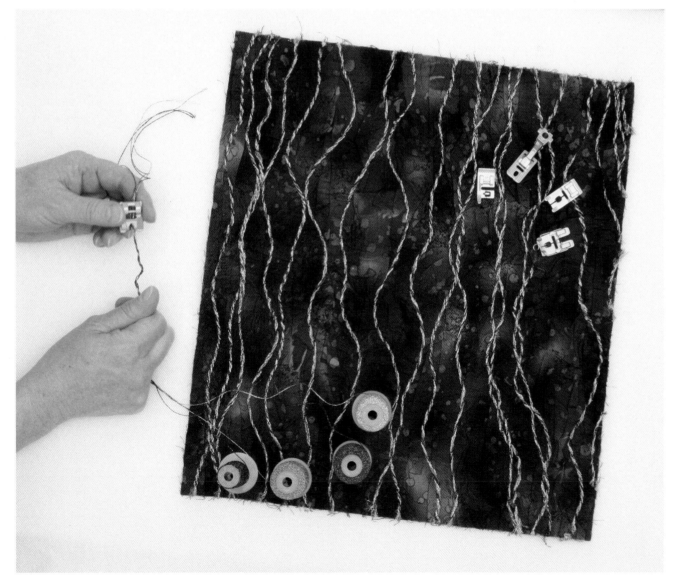

tips:

• *Adjust the stitch width to fit the twisted threads. If the needle thread misses the couching threads, enlarge the width. If the needle thread extends off the couching thread, shorten the stitch width.*

• *Use decorative stitches for couching, too. Be sure the stitch you choose enhances the design instead of hiding it. Move the stitch forward at angles to prevent matting the couched threads.*

• *Avoid pull by swinging the needle over the couching threads rather than piercing them.*

Most people tend to match colors too well, so use contrasting colors for visibility. Try using thread colors you would never buy in fabric. Notice the sparkle the lime green adds to the twisted purple, blue and pink!

Choose the foot with the hole closest to the size of the couching threads to maintain proper alignment. Some feet have an adjustable screw to alter the size of the hole.

The multi-hole or groove-cording foot, with its different holes, grooves or slots, aligns the couching thread perfectly and keeps it in the same position while stitching. The different holes create the illusion of a ribbon. Using practical or decorative stitches can produce neat special effects. The honeycomb stitch is fun to use with the multi-hole foot.

Play with the decorative stitches on your machine. I haven't found anyone yet who has used all the stitches on their machine.

Slide the couching threads through the holes on the foot. Once they are threaded, tie them into a knot before attaching the foot to the machine. This prevents the threads from loosening from the foot before you are ready to stitch.

Ordinarily, all holes in the foot are threaded at once. But even though there are a number of holes in a foot, you do not have to use them all at the same time. Use only the outer holes with a decorative stitch to the maximum width; use odd holes to leave space between the lines of couching threads; or incorporate a variety of uses with the same foot into one project. Every stitched row can be a different application.

Ribbon floss is a bias-woven ribbon. Spread the end, and pull one of the fibers to gather the ribbon.

Ruching creates elegant texture. Use the open-toe embroidery foot or open-toe appliqué foot to apply the gathered ribbon. Don't catch the loops in the foot. Use an open decorative stitch, like the entredeux or little daisy stitch.

tip:

Tie a knot in one end of the ribbon floss and gather to the knot, keeping the pulled thread loose. Begin stitching by the knot, and continue toward the pulled thread. You can shift the floss threads if so desired. Do not cut the gathered thread until the ruched ribbon has been applied to the fabric.

Ribbon Floss

Strip-Piecing Option

There are many basic strip-piecing patterns that transfer well to handbags.
Strip piecing is a variation of log cabin in the quilting world or chevron in the sewing world.

The piecing begins with a triangle shape at the open edge of the bag. I have included two pattern pieces — the Triangle Top (#11) for a narrow opening and Triangle Bottom (#12) for a wide opening.

Choose the main fabric in the project for the triangle, side panels, strap, gusset and pockets, and choose five or more other fabrics to include in the piecing. The amount of fabric you will need for each strip will differ. You may use some strips only once, while others may be repeated several times. A collection of fat quarters to go along with the dominant fabric is usually sufficient; and of course, a small bag requires less fabric than a large one.

Use a rotary cutter and ruler to cut strips for the piecing. Vary the width of the strips to add character to the project. You may choose to use a favorite fabric several times in different widths. Strips should be cut from 1¼" to 2½" wide. A ¼" seam allowance is taken from each side of the strip in the piecing process so that the finished strips become ¾" to 2". Cut the widths of the strips in proportion to the size of your handbag. A small bag will look better with narrow strips, while a large bag can have a combination of wide and narrow strips. Use varying widths of fabric.

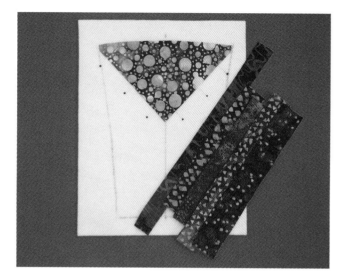

1 Begin with a fleece base that is slightly larger than the Center Panel (#1). Using a fabric marker and ruler for accuracy, draw a straight line down the center length of the fleece to use as a guide. Place the triangle right side up on the fleece at the upper center edge, and work outward. If using fusible fleece, steam the triangle to the fleece. If using basic fleece, pin or baste the triangle in place.

2 Place the first strip on the triangle with right sides together. Keeping the cut edges even and using a ¼" seam allowance, stitch the length of the strip. Use a stitch length of 2.5 to 3 to piece on the fleece. This stitching will show on the other side of the fleece.

3 Turn the strip over to expose the right side of the strip and the triangle. Lightly press to hold the added strip to the fleece.

tip:

Every machine has an optional ¼" foot. This foot is designed to stitch accurate ¼" seam allowances, a popular size for piecing. Some machines have an additional bar attached to the right side of the foot to align with the cut edge of the fabric — both feet makes it easy to stitch perfect ¼" seam allowances every time.

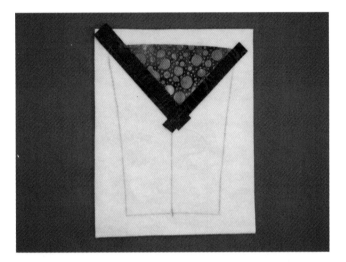

4 Attach the next strip the same way, at an approximate right angle to the first strip and triangle. Be sure that the strip extends from the point and past the fleece.

5 Turn the strip over to expose the right side of the strip and the triangle. Lightly press to hold the added strip to the fleece. Once you understand how the sequence works, it is okay to trim excess fabric strips.

tip:

Be careful as you press — don't touch the iron to the fusible.

6 Working on alternate sides, follow the stitch-and-flip method until the fleece is completely covered. Trim the chevron piece to the desired handbag size, and continue making the bag.

Stitching will show on the wrong side of the fleece.

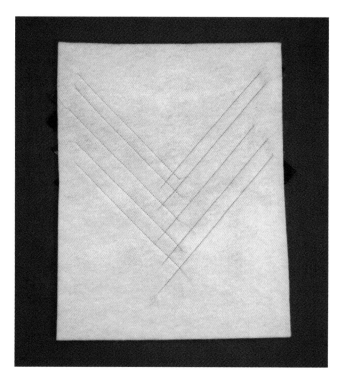

tip:

To avoid cutting the strip too short, always trim extra fabric strips after flipping the strip.

hints:

- *Establish a piecing system, or make it up as you go.*

- *Cut the strips the same width consistently, or vary the widths.*

- *Use narrow strips for accent colors. Use wider strips to fill.*

- *When a strip has been cut a little too wide, move the needle position rather than trimming the strip. No one will notice the wider seam allowance.*

You may need extra support for a large bag. To add more weight, bond a layer of muslin to the underside of the fleece before piecing.

other uses for triangle top (#11) and triangle bottom (#12)

The triangle shape is an opportunity to show embroidery. This arcing design is actually the letter L repeated several times.

To cut the triangle shape exactly the way you want it, work with a window as shown rather than covering the design with the pattern. Copy the shape of the pattern. Use the small rotary cutter to cut the desired size from the pattern, being careful to keep the outside edges intact. Place the window over the embroidery design. Include space for the ¼" seam allowance on all sides. Mark the fabric, and trim to size.

flap

Use the Triangle Top (#11) and Triangle Bottom (#12) as a flap for the bag. Determine which shape is proper for your bag. The design of #11 is more vertical, whereas #12 is more horizontal. Choose the flap that is attractive and compatible with the bag's other embellishments or pockets.

Double-faced quilted fabric was used for these flaps. Bind the edge of the triangle on the two identical sides. The remaining edge is included in the finishing of the opening.

The large bag with gusset using the Triangle Bottom (#12)

Bag without flap

Use leftovers from a larger project to make the small bag with flap.

Finishing Detail

Corded piping, a narrow strip of bias fabric containing a cord, adds a nice finishing touch to a handbag. It is one of my favorite trims, and it can be metallic, shiny, plaid, striped, big, small, double, contrast or blend.

A purchased decorative corded piping can enhance your design. Corded piping is available in basic fabric or decorative patterns in small packages or by the yard. Look in home decoration as well as fashion fabric stores — both types of stores usually offer a wide range of color and texture.

Sometimes you will need to make your own corded piping to match or contrast with your handbag. Traditionally, bias is used for corded piping. However, because fabric gives on the crosswise grain, you can use the crosswise grain when trimming areas that are relatively straight.

Different sizes of cord will require different amounts of fabric. For small to medium corded piping, the bias strips should be 1¼" wide. For larger cording, the bias strips may need to be 1½" wide.

This technique is easier if you use a foot designed specifically for cording.

tip:

Quilt shops offer bias binding by the yard, which is suitable for making corded piping.

tip:

With a stripe or plaid, always use bias for effect. Sometimes you can use cross-cut strips, and the way a stripe or plaid is printed on the fabric may determine how it should be cut, too.

Position the cording in the center of the fabric strip. Fold the fabric in half over the cord. Keeping the cut edges together, place the cording under the ridge or tunnel in the foot.

For very small cording, use the largest pintucking foot. Change the needle position to stitch close to the cording, but do not go too close. The bias fabric will eventually be stitched three times, so use a longer stitch length to avoid getting a build-up of stitches. Each stitching will be closer to the cording, making the final stitching the closest to the cord. Move the needle position so the previous rows of stitching don't show.

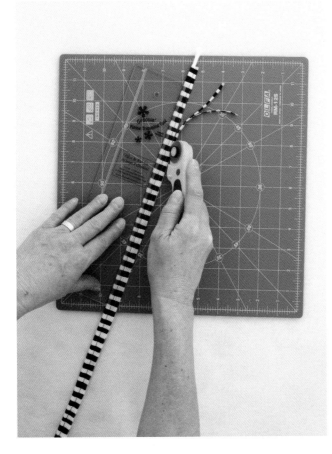

It is difficult to cut corded piping the perfect width. I've discovered a wonderful tool designed specifically for this purpose — and sometimes spending a little money is worth saving valuable time. Cut the bias strip slightly wider than necessary, and make the corded piping. The seam allowance will be slightly larger than the desired ¼". Then, use the Groovin' Piping Trimming Tool to trim the excess fabric away from the seam allowance. The cord fits in the groove under the ruler. Use the rotary cutter to trim the seam allowance to a perfect ¼". It couldn't be easier! The ruler tool was designed for small corded piping, but it works for large corded piping, too.

Too much corded piping at the seam intersections will cause extra bulk, which may be eliminated by pulling and trimming the cording from the seam allowance where the corded piping enters a crossing seam.

After trimming, run your finger over the corded piping to relax the cord.

hints:

- *Consider using several sizes of corded piping in one bag to add variety. ¹/₈" and ¹/₄" are good sizes, depending on the bag.*

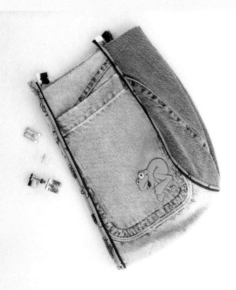

- *For variation, use double-corded piping in a variety of sizes and colors.*

tips:

- *Fine-tuning the last detail will result in a professional-looking bag.*

- *Use a double layer of bias fabric on coarsely-twisted cord to prevent the ridges in the cord from showing through the bias binding.*

Striped fabric for corded piping could be cut on the crosswise grain or the bias.

The bias of faux suede is generally the cross-grain of the fabric. Double-check the stretch before cutting. Faux suede is a relatively inexpensive trim, and it's very durable, doesn't ravel, is washable and combines well with fabrics like tapestry, denim and pillow ticking.

It is better to have too much fabric on the corded piping and trim the excess than have too little fabric, because it is awkward to work with a narrow strip of corded piping.

Use the piping tool to trim the seam allowance to a perfect ¼". The tool is accurate every time. For best results, use a piping foot to attach corded piping. The size of the groove in the foot correlates directly to the size of the cord.

Change the needle position to stitch closer to the piping and make a snug fit.

For an alternative to corded piping, use a zipper. Two 20" zippers equals 80" of cording.

magnetic snap closure

There are a variety of magnetic snap closures that will give your handbag a professional-looking finish. Some are stitched to the lining of the bag. Others are inserted with a pair of needle-nose pliers. I recommend keeping a pair of pliers with your sewing equipment so they stay clean.

When you look at ready-to-wear handbags, you will often see magnetic snaps used to hold flaps in place. The snaps are purchased in a set with a male and female part and two metal support pieces. There are several sizes, colors and types of magnetic snaps available.

Choose the style that complements your bag.

---

tip:

A magnetic snap secures the opening of the bag and makes it look like a purchased handbag.

magnetic snap with prongs

Determine where the snap should be placed on the handbag lining center panel — usually it will be just below the center point from the opening. Position the prongs on the back of the snap on the right side of the fabric. Push the prongs into the fabric to mark position. The prongs are generally not sharp enough to push through the fabric, so use a very sharp, pointed small scissors or the point of a button cutter set to cut a slash for the prongs to slide through.

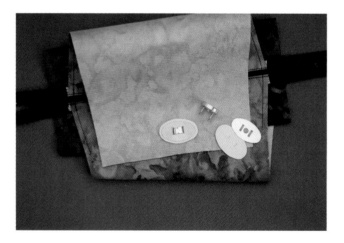

To prevent the metal support piece of the magnetic snap set from cutting the fabric, place a piece of thin, laminated cardboard or plastic template over the metal prongs on the wrong side of the fabric. This cardboard or plastic piece should be slightly larger than the metal support piece. Slide the metal support piece over the cardboard. Use pliers to bend the prongs flat over the metal support piece. Make sure the prongs are flat so they won't puncture the lining or the bag later.

Magnetic snaps are available in multiple colors. Choose the color that best suits your bag — the color of the snap should not detract from the rest of the bag.

It is best to attach the snap after stitching the lining to the bag, so you can position the snap properly. If you place the snap on the lining before the lining is attached, the snap may be placed too high, making it impossible to stitch the lining without the pressure foot touching the snap.

sew-in magnetic snap

A new variety of magnetic snap has a ridge surrounding the magnetic center and four sets of holes to stitch the snap in place.

Position the snap on the fabric just below the center point of the lining. It is always a good idea to add an extra layer of stabilizer to the lining by the snap. This secures the stitching and makes the lining fabric more durable. Using the holes in the snap, stitch the snap directly to the lining fabric.

tip:

Choose the right size magnetic snap for your bag. Magnetic snaps come in sizes from ½" to ¾".

Use two magnetic snaps on larger bags or totes.

Instead of stitching the sew-in magnetic snap directly to the lining, you can make a lining pocket to hold the magnetic snap. My first idea was to apply a facing to the wrong side of the lining for the snap. I used the wavy blade from the rotary cutter set to cut the fabric, and I stitched a small piece of curved fabric slightly larger than the snap to the wrong side of the lining to form a pocket.

It was difficult to stitch a nice curve on such a small piece of fabric, so in other bags, I applied a straight strip of fabric to the opening portion of the lining. A box shape holds the facing layers together, and a straight line is much easier to stitch than a curve.

Stitch whichever line you prefer.
Use the wavy blade with the rotary cutter to cut the facing piece. This prevents a ridge from forming on the lining side as the bag is worn, much like trimming with pinking shears on a seam allowance. Before stitching the snap in place or sliding the snap in the fabric pocket, make sure the magnetic parts are facing each other properly.

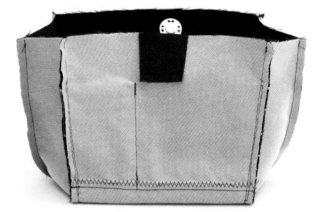

other hardware ideas

There are other hardware options for organizing your bag.

A swivel snap may be attached to the inside or outside of the bag.

Use belting or the handle loop to attach the swivel in the upper portion of the bag, close to the top. Use a swivel on each side of the bag if you choose. Swivels should be placed on diagonal corners from each other to balance the weight and prevent rubbing against each other.

Straps & Handles

Your bag will need some type of strap, chain or handle. There are unlimited possibilities for choosing a strap. Study the bags in this book for creative ways to "handle" the strap situation.

Various pattern pieces are given for the appropriate sizes of the bags — use Strap (#3), Button and Chain Loop (#10) or Handle Loop (#14). Straps are an easy alteration, but plan before cutting. Decide which style, type, length and width you want. A strap is long and worn over the shoulder. A handle is short and designed to be carried in the hand. Sometimes a chain may be appropriate — it's up to you.

The strap in this pattern is 44" long, but you can shorten or lengthen it as desired. Consider how you plan to wear the bag. If you need extra length, find out before cutting the fabric. Use a tape measure as a strap for testing purposes.

Smaller bags require a narrower strap than larger totes. The width of the strap should be in direct proportion to the size of the bag. Choose a strap that complements the handbag and is comfortable to carry. A double strap or handle works well for a bag with a wide opening, and a longer strap is more suitable for a bag with a narrow top. Be creative! Even an old belt could become a strap.

Whenever possible, cut strap fabric on the length of the fabric. Woven fabric gives on the crosswise grain, but not on the lengthwise grain. Wide straps should be cut on the lengthwise grain. You can cut narrow straps on the crosswise grain. Interfacing may be necessary for added support or strength, depending on the fabric.

To save time and money, keep a 45"-long piece of interfacing handy and labeled for straps. Make sure that this piece is the lengthwise grain of the interfacing. Knit interfacing stretches on the crosswise grain.

Always double stitch a strap for durability. Decorative stitching is another possibility.

We all use leftovers for smaller projects, and sometimes there is not enough length to make a strap. If you need extra length, join the fabric pieces together with a seam line cut at a 45-degree angle. In the folding process, the seam line will be evenly distributed.

To lengthen a cut strap, use a D-ring or other decorative hardware between the short pieces of strap.

tip:

Use a chain for small handbags or evening bags. Use a strap on everyday bags and larger totes. Choose a decorative handle for a small handbag.

traditional straps

To begin, determine how long the strap should be, judging by the way it is worn. A strap positioned on the shoulder and dropping down toward the hipline is shorter than a strap worn on one shoulder, crossing the body to the hip on the other side. Determine which you prefer. You can also make the strap adjustable, or tie a knot in a narrow strap to shorten it.

When I first began to make handbags, straps seemed very simple — I would stitch a tube of fabric and turn it. For very soft fabrics, this was a good solution, but it didn't work for every fabric. Lightweight fabrics were often too soft to make a durable handle, and heavy tapestries, double faced quilted fabrics and denim were extremely difficult to turn. The fabric was too heavy, causing lumps and bumps that looked amateurish. After playing with a variety of materials, I discovered various solutions for light and heavy fabrics.

One strap technique uses four layers of fabric. As a test, fold your fabric to four thicknesses to determine if this is the proper strap technique. If the fabric is too soft, stabilize it with a lightweight interfacing. Sometimes it is better to interface a portion of the strap rather than the whole fabric piece.

1 Fold the fabric in half lengthwise and press with wrong sides together. Open the strip and press the outside cut edges almost to the center foldline. There should be a slight ⅛" space between the cut edges.

2 Fold in half along the original pressed foldline. With the edge-stitching foot aligned next to the open edge first, move the needle position to the desired distance from the fold, and stitch the open side closed.

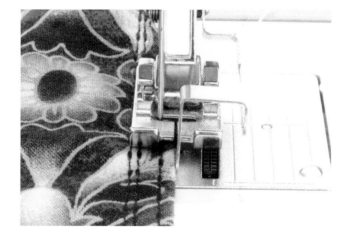

3 Stitch the remaining edge, so that both edges are stitched evenly. For added decoration, stitch several other rows of either straight or decorative stitches.

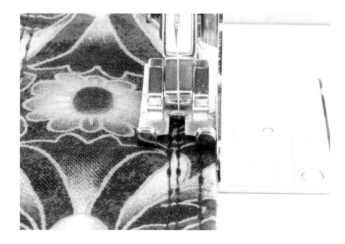

heavyweight fabric straps

Heavy fabric, like denim, faux suede and double-faced quilted fabric, is too bulky and stiff to use four layers of fabric in a strap. To use these fabrics, first determine the desired finished width, and then double that amount. Cut the fabric this width — there are no seam allowances.

1 Position a fusing medium on the full width and length of the wrong side of the fabric.

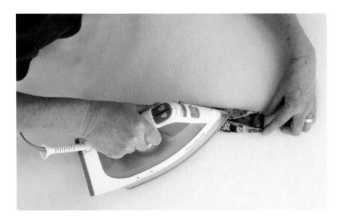

2 Fold the outside edges to the center, and fuse the layers together using the wool setting on a steam iron.

3 Edge stitch or top stitch each edge of the strap for durability.

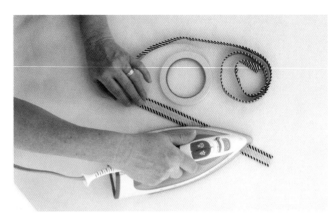

If you are using faux suede, the exposed cut edge is a finished edge. Other fabrics can ravel and cause an unsightly mess, so cover the two cut edges with a bias trim. To make it easier to position the trim proportionally over the cut edges of the strap, place a fusing medium on the back of the trim.

One of my favorite products is Steam-a-Seam by the roll. It is sticky, which allows me to position the applied fabric where I want it.

If you change your mind, lift and reposition the trim. The trim is not final until it is heat-set and stitched in place.

tip:

Cover the raw edges of tapestries with faux suede. Use ribbon or braiding as an alternative.

A measuring tape was just the thing to enhance the strap for these sewing ladies.

Insert rick rack between the layers of trim and strap for decorative appeal.

Use bias plaid or stripe to add variety.

Shop for straps in the home décor department. Drapery pullbacks make exquisite straps.

Braid purchased decorative cord to make a strap.

Make a strap out of recycled jewelry or decorative beads.

adjustable strap with webbing

Webbing or belting makes an easy, quick strap. Width and color variety may be limited, but matching hardware is available to enhance the style or make an adjustable strap. You will need a D-ring and slider for adjustable straps. A short strap length of about 6" slides through the D-ring. This double thickness of strap is secured to the handbag. The main length of strap is secured to the slider, a rectangular metal or plastic part with a crossbar in the center. Attach the strap to the center crossbar, so the top of the slider and the seam allowance are facing up.

Slip the belting through the D-ring, and weave it through the slider. The strap comes under the outside edge, over the crossbar on top of the seam allowance that attaches the strap to the slider, and under the other outside edge. The strap continues through the shoulder strap, if desired, and attaches to the opposite side of the bag.

tip:

Attach a D-ring and slider to each end to make them both adjustable.

When making a strap of nylon or polyester belting, use a soldering iron to melt or seal the ends of the belting and prevent it from raveling.

Use a shoulder pad to distribute the weight of heavier bags.

using chain as a strap

Chain can be used with small, light handbags or evening bags. Chains on large,

heavy bags could hurt your shoulder.

For decorative purposes, weave suede, leather, yarn or ribbon through a chain. Weaving may shorten the chain length, so be certain to weave the chain before cutting extra length. Chanel is known for using chain this way.

Many chains suitable for handbags have very small interlocking links. To attach the chain to the bag, add a double split jump ring to the last link. This ring is a tiny key ring — it slides onto the chain and slips around and around until it is secure.

The jump ring is large enough to accommodate a fabric loop stitched to the bag. Use a fabric loop rather than just stitching for support to hold the weight of the bag. My favorite fabric loop is made like a belt loop (or like the strap). Use the Button and Chain Loop (#10) folded like the strap, only narrower. Cut the pattern piece longer than necessary so you have something to hold onto. Most of the time, the stitching on such a small piece isn't very pretty — with the added length, you can throw away the excess. You only need two 1½" strips for each end of the chain.

Slip the fabric loop through the double split jump ring, leaving it longer at this point. To attach the chain to the handbag, stagger the ends rather than laying them on top of each other. This spreads the weight on the loops and gets rid of unnecessary bulk. When you start to stitch, place the needle in the center of the loop, stitch forward and then stitch backward to hold in place. If you begin at the edge of the loop, it will generally slip from underneath the foot, and you'll have to start over. Stitch the chain at the side seams of the bag.

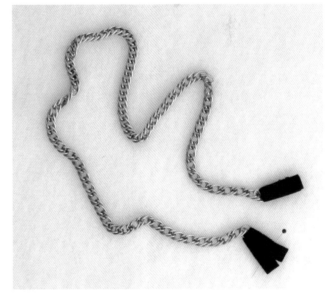

tip:

You can stitch drapery tiebacks with loops on each end to the bag using the Button and Chain Loop (#10).

Use decorative handles rather than fabric handles for additional pizzazz. Most decorative handles have a large ring incorporated into the design to attach it to the bag. Use Handle Loop #14 to attach a decorative handle. Construct the handle loop like the fabric strap, using four layers of folded fabric. If you use a lightweight fabric, use interfacing for added support. Attach the handle the same way as the chain — it will just be wider.

If you need to change the width of the fabric loop, measure the opening in the handle and multiply it by four.

Use two handles for short, hand-held bags, not shoulder handles. Attach the handles next to the center panel seam allowances — do not place the handle loops on top of the corded piping, or it will be bulky.

tip:

Stagger the ends of the handle loop while attaching it to the bag to eliminate bulk in the side seam.

Double-Faced Quilted Fabric

Double-faced quilted fabric is lined as it is cut out, which is a timesaver from the start.
You can decide which fabric is the outside and which is the inside of the bag.
Switch it up with different panel pieces for style.

Because everyone's schedule is so full, sewing projects should be quick and fun to make. Working with double-faced quilted fabric lets you take some shortcuts. There are some wonderful quilted fabrics that work nicely for handbags. Make a small bag in minutes to jazz up your summer or holiday wardrobe, and use a large bag with gusset for commuting, going to the gym or taking a weekend vacation.

A companion fabric is necessary for corded piping and binding. Choose a solid color, print, striped or plaid fabric to blend or contrast.

tip:

Use a serger or the over-cast stitch on the machine to finish the edges. Some seams are finished with binding. Some seams could be stitched together before finishing the edge, while others are easier to finish in a single layer. Because this is a quick project, seam allowances are visible on the inside.

the large bag with a gusset

It is impossible to make a secret pocket for the small, medium and large bags;

however, it is very easy to make a secret pocket for the gusset.

the secret pocket in the gusset

1 With the right side of the zipper facing the right side of the fabric, attach the zipper to the secret pocket for large with gusset (#8). Allow the zipper to extend on both ends of the pocket piece. Position the all-purpose foot next to the zipper coil, with the needle in the far left position. Stitch the length of the zipper.

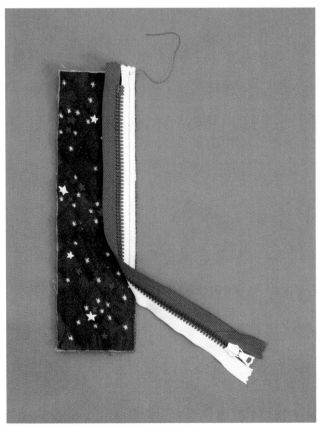

3 Attach the other half of the pocket in the same manner.

2 Roll the fabric away from the zipper coil. Position the edge-stitching foot on the zipper coil, with the bar on the foot lined between the fold of the fabric and the zipper coil. Move the needle position to the left several notches, and edge stitch the fold.

4 Bind the short ends of the secret pocket. Stitch and finish the seam allowance at the bottom of the gusset. Center this pocket over the seam allowance. Baste the long edges to the gusset, and trim excess pocket fabric along the length.

tip:

Use leftover zipper tape rather than binding to cover the raw ends of the zipper.

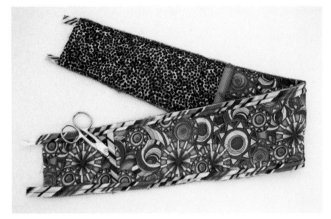

5 Make the gusset panel pockets in the same manner as the traditional bag by bringing the notched dotted foldline to match the solid notched line. Bind the edge of the pocket if desired. Baste the layers of seam allowances to hold the pocket in place. To finish, serge or over cast the layers on the long edges of the gusset.

6 Apply corded piping to both long edges of the gusset piece.

inside pockets

1 Because the quilted fabric is already doubled, you don't need to double it to make a pocket. Cut one pocket of the pleated patch pocket for lining (#9) to make two. In other words, fold the pattern along the first foldline for the new pattern piece to make the lining patch pocket. You can also cut one pocket and divide it in half to make two.

2 Finish one long edge of the inside pleated patch pocket with binding and the other with the over-cast stitch.

3 Form the pleat by matching the foldline to the centerline.

4 Determine whether the bag should have a wide or narrow opening. Position the pocket on the lining, and stitch in place.

5 Fold the pocket to form a small pleat at the bottom for more room.

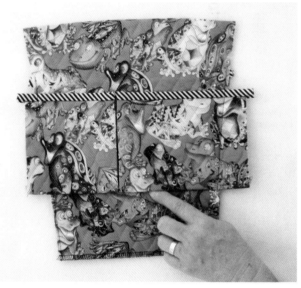

6 Stitch down the center of the pleat to make two pockets rather than one.

outside patch pocket option

If you want a patch pocket on the outside of the bag, use the fashion fabric center panel (#1), with the upper edge trimmed away approximately 2".

1 Bind the upper edge.

2 Layer the pocket over the center panel, trim excess and finish the outside edges.

3 Attach the lining pockets before attaching the outside pockets, so the outside pocket stitching covers the lining pockets. Be sure the inside pockets and outside pockets are staggered in layers, so you don't have bulky seam allowances.

tip:

Cut the outside patch pocket with a slight curve or slant for variety.

outside pleated pocket option

Because the quilted fabric is doubled in the beginning, it is not necessary to double it to make a pocket.

1 Cut one pocket of the outside pleated patch pocket pattern (#13) to make two. Divide the fabric along the first foldline.

2 Form the inverted pleat at the upper edge of the pocket, making it half the size of the original pleat. Omit the inverted pleat at the lower edge. Determine which side should show on the outside of the pocket. Form the pleats at the side of each corner to make the rounded corners.

3 Bind the edges of the pocket.

4 Begin stitching the binding along the straight edge of the sides, leaving the first few inches where the binding is cut at a slant loose. Stretch the binding slightly as the machine reaches the curves. It appears slightly warped now, but the finished pocket will be flat.

5 Stitch off the edge of the corner. Fold the binding back to form a right angle. You may need to pull slightly on the binding to stretch the last few stitches so the angle is smooth, but do not cut the stitches.

6 Fold the binding back on top of itself to make a square corner.

7 Begin stitching at the corner.

8 When you reach the beginning point, trim excess binding at an angle. Be extremely careful not to trim too much. Tuck the end into the beginning. Stitch to attach the binding completely around the outside edge of the pocket.

9 Pull the binding away from the pocket, and fold it over the cut edge to encase it.

10 Stitch in the ditch to hold the binding in place. Position the pocket on the center panel, and stitch in the ditch a second time to hold the pocket on the bag.

Warning: The stitching on the outside pocket will form additional sections on the lining pocket.

tip:

Because quilted fabric is so heavy, the pleat at the upper edge should be made smaller and the pleat at the lower edge should be omitted.

outside zipper pocket

1 Cut a piece of fabric slightly larger than the center panel (#1). Choose your outside fabric. Cut the fabric horizontally or at a slant, with the upper cut about 2" from the top. Insert the zipper with the ends extending on both ends. Use the same zipper technique used to insert the zipper on the gusset secret pocket.

2 Place the zipper pocket on top of another center panel. Baste and finish the edges.

3 Apply the corded piping to each side of the center panel.

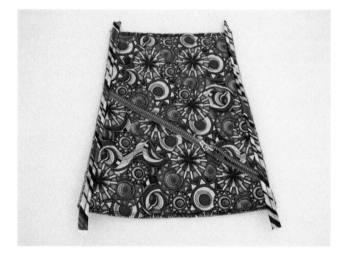

4 Attach the side panels to the center panel.

5 Attach the center panels to the gusset. It is easiest to finish the edges before you combine the layers because of the bulk of the fabric.

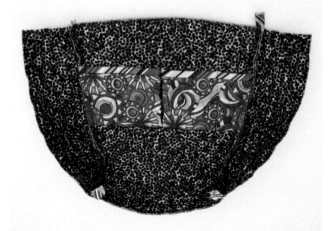

tip:

Using the narrow end of the center panel at the bottom of the bag causes the gusset to be slightly long. After pinning and stitching the gusset to the center panels, trim the excess. This should be approximately 1" on each end of the gusset.

4 Use binding to finish the raw edge at the opening of the bag.

5 Choose the strap style for the bag you have created. Refer to the Straps and Handles chapter for suggestions. Attach the straps on the lining side of the side seams or the gusset, depending on the bag size. The straps are not encased in a seam allowance. Double stitch the straps for security.

other bags without a gusset

The instructions for making the other size bags without a gusset vary slightly.

1 Stitch the notched seam line of the side panels.
Finish the edges.

2 Attach desired pockets on the lining, and stitch
the bottom seam. Finish the edges.

3 Attach desired pockets on the outside of the
bag. Add corded piping to each side.

4 Stitch the side panels to the center panel. Use
binding at the opening, and attach the straps.
Refer to the Straps and Handles chapter for
suggestions.

tip:

Use surplus fabric to make a matching
wallet, smaller bag, jewelry bag, CD
case or eyeglass case.

Changing the Pattern

With the popularity of embroidery, quilting, pillow blocks and printer fabrics, it's easy to find an insert — but it may not be the right size! Sometimes a pattern is too small for a special fabric insert — or a design is too large for a pattern. Luckily, there are solutions to the problem, so you can make almost any pattern work for your handbag.

enlarging the pattern

Choose the pattern size that matches the insert as closely as possible. To enlarge the pattern, begin by tracing the original size. Slash the main pattern piece, center panel (#1), on the grain line. Use graph paper for accuracy, or mark a plain sheet of paper with a ruler.

Tape the pattern to the graph paper, matching lines for precision. Add the appropriate number of inches to the pattern. Use the lines on the graph paper to keep the pattern pieces aligned properly and determine how much to add.

Alter any pattern pieces that come in contact with the original piece. For example, the lining and pockets are affected by adding to the center panel (#1).

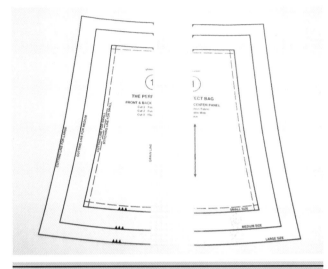

tip:

Check and double-check to make sure the pattern pieces match.

Be sure to include seam allowances. When ¼" seam allowances are necessary for a project, they must be included in the cutting plans.

The Hear No Evil, See No Evil, Speak No Evil frogs were originally printed on a T-shirt. In order to use them on this pattern, 4" were added to the center panel (#1) of the large pattern.

The Counted XS design was slightly large for the small pattern using the wider opening. To make the design fit, 1" was added to the center panel.

The same Counted XS design in other colorations works well on the medium bag with a narrow opening. The center panel width is not altered.

hints:

- *Always keep the original pattern intact as a master. Any time the pattern requires altering, trace the original and change the affected pieces. Maintain a labeled folder for each size and altered pattern for easy reference. I keep each pattern size in a zipped plastic bag labeled with the appropriate changes.*

- *Keep a tablet of ¼" graph paper convenient in the sewing room. It will come in handy for alterations.*

- *Use removable blue-plaid tape to alter paper pattern pieces, so it is easy to reposition pieces when necessary without tearing the paper.*

filling in a small insert

Sometimes it is necessary to enlarge a small insert until it is big enough for a bag. Study the focal piece and ask yourself: How big would I like this piece to be? How much do I need to add before I lose my insert? What do I have in my collection to use with this piece? What combination will make it look like this project was planned this way from the beginning?

The Sewphisticates panel print from Loralie Designs would make an adorable handbag, but the panel is too small to stand alone. The panel is almost wide enough, but you would need more length to finish the bottom of the bag.

The first step is to decide whether the opening should be wide or narrow. It looks like either would be fine with this insert.

1 Cut a piece of fusible fleece that is slightly larger than the center panel (#1). Place the fusible side up.

2 Position the panel on the fleece at the upper portion of the fleece, with the right side of the panel facing up. Make sure the panel is straight on the fleece. Steam the layers together to hold the panel in place.

3 To make the piping, cut a strip of companion fabric 1¼" wide and slightly longer than the width of the panel. Press the length of this strip with wrong sides together, making the strip ⅝" wide.

4 Position the folded edge of the piping along the bottom edge of the panel where it looks best. Shift the piping several times around the bottom of the design to determine the right spot. The folded edge of the piping should face the design, and the cut edge of the piping should face the cut edge of the design. The cut edges may be staggered.

5 Using a longer stitch length, about 3½ to 4, baste in place.

6 Cut another piece of fabric the width of the fleece and the length necessary to fill in the remaining fleece. Be sure to include extra fabric for seam allowances — trim the excess later.

7 Place the cut edge of this fabric along the cut edge of the piping fabric. Study the size of the piping to determine how much should be visible on the finished project. Sometimes ⅛" looks best — other times, ¼" is more appropriate. This design element will be different for each project.

8 Stitch the layers together using a stitch length of 3. If you can't decide which width to use, choose a longer stitch length for a trial run.

tip:

Don't worry about the seam allowance at the piping seam. Sometimes seam allowances in the design area may differ from seam allowances in the construction area — that's okay. What is important is the visible area of the design, because no one will see underneath.

Using ⅝" folded piping allows you to make the finished visible piping edge anywhere from ¹⁄₁₆" to ⅜". For best results, cut and press piping accurately. The cut edge of the piping is the guide for stitching. Beginning with uneven piping affects the layout of future seams, so precision is important.

Use corded piping as an alternative. The size of the corded piping will be determined by the style of your insert and the size of your bag.

Should less piping be necessary, make the seam allowance wider and examine the results. Make adjustments accordingly. Once the fabric addition is stitched in place, trim the excess seam allowance if necessary, and flip the fabric addition to show the combination. Steam the layers to form the center panel.

Study the panel with the pattern in hand, and choose a wide or narrow opening. You must also decide whether to use a ¼" traditional seam allowance or binding.

Usually a ⅜" seam allowance is designed for 1¼" binding. ⅛" doesn't seem like much fabric, but that small amount could make a big difference. In this case, it determined whether the hair was trimmed off or the white background continued to frame the lady.

Once you decide, center the pattern over the fabric, and cut the panel accordingly.

tip:

Always check and double-check before trimming.

I decided to make a bag with each opening option. For the first bag, I outlined the panel with medium rick rack for additional flair. I chose red, the dominant color in both panels. A narrow opening completed the look.

The second bag, using more Sewphisticates, was trimmed with rainbow rick rack. Using the wider opening at the top exposed a portion of the black-and-white panel trim. To cover the unwanted trim, the rick rack was moved slightly toward the center. This exposed too much rick rack for the design, so plaid piping on the bias filled in that area and became part of the design.

The tiger's eyes made a nice addition to a handbag. The embroidery was wide enough for the center panel, but it was too small to stand alone. A wonderful jungle print created the illusion of the tiger's eyes staring through the leaves. Notice how the eyes appear on the front of the bag with zebra piping compared to the back of the bag with solely jungle print.

1 To begin this project, cut fusible fleece slightly larger than the center panel pattern. Place fusible side up.

2 Position the embroidery slightly higher than center on the fleece. Steam in place. Add piping along the top and bottom edge of the embroidery.

3 Fill the remaining space with jungle fabric. Cut the design to fit the pattern, and continue making the bag.

tip:

Understand the shape of the finished bag before inserting a panel. The Perfect Bag has round-shaped side panels, which form the bottom of the bag and give it width. The center panel becomes a portion of the bottom of the bag, too. The vertical middle of the center panel piece is not the center of the finished bag. The center of the panel, in respect to a focal point or inset, is higher on the pattern — so keep the design high on the bag rather than allowing the design to fall toward the bottom of the bag.

altering the style

Some things that happen by mistake can become a new design — like making lemonade from lemons. That's how the bottom became the top and the top became the bottom of this bag. One day I wasn't paying close attention, and I stitched the top first. The side panels fit, so there was no problem. When the bag was finished, I realized that now I had two styles! One was wider at the top, and the other was wider at the bottom.

Something very interesting happened with the side panels, too. The side panel (#2) pattern has a double notch on the side that should be stitched first. For the fun of it, I stitched the long, curved edge first instead.

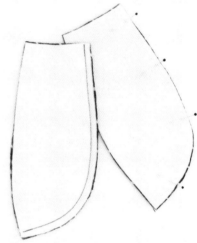

The pieces almost fit, but the center panel was a little too long. Well, I just cut the excess off, applied the same instruction to the lining — and now I had a new pattern!

Each of these bags was stitched so the outer edges were curved rather than round.

hint:

It is okay to mix, match and play with patterns. If you discover a new style, hurrah! Write down the changes so you remember the new design shape. After all, creativity is why we sew.

Gallery from a Challenge

I always like to work with a basic pattern and play. Once the pattern is perfected, it's easy to give it an entirely different appearance by changing the decoration — this is true for handbags as well.

A challenge was presented at www.ghees. com to create a handbag using a basic pattern. Entrants chose the size, fabric and decoration. As the bags arrived, it was obvious that each bag had a story to tell. Some seemed to be completely different, but each bag was made from the same multi-sized pattern.

Study the bags, and note how each designer brought her own artistic vision to the bag. Consider the "things" that are in your sewing room.

Rethink how and where you shop. It's well worth dipping into the collection with a new attitude. Some products that were designed for one purpose have multiple uses. For instance, a button was designed to fasten or act as a closure — but a collection of buttons can also a beautiful focal point or embellishment.

Study these bags, and bring your own personality into your next handbag project:

"Inspiration from Three Dear Friends"
Suzanne D. Winkler • Katy, Texas
This bag was first place.

"I enjoy creating purses with a special person in mind using fabrics and embellishments that are meaningful to both of us," Suzanne Winkler said. She has been making purses for friends and family for some time, usually incorporating crazy quilting. Suzanne loves the creativity of embellishing purses, and each bag comes out differently. She has collected fabrics and trims through the years, and she is always looking for new materials with a meaningful history. She draws from her collection of beads and jewelry to make the beaded handles, and to personalize her purses, Suzanne adds a picture to the inside pocket. This photo of Suzanne, with her friends from kindergarten, Deidra and Gerry, was taken at a reunion just before Hurricane Katrina. They grew up in New Orleans and have stayed friends even though they live in three different states. "Inspiration from Three Dear Friends" is a reminder of their friendship.

"Purple Passion Pocket Pouch Purse"
Marie Stefani • Adamsburg, PA
This bag was second place.

When it's time to recycle that old winter coat, consider felting the wool and making a handbag! Washing wool in hot water and putting it in the dryer makes the fabric denser and suitable for a handbag. Marie Stefani made the inserts for her purse using Fay Maxwell's slash and burn technique. They were appliquéd to the felt using a decorative machine stitch with variegated embroidery thread. Many, many hand-stitched seed beads accent the opening edge and flap. Additional hand-stitched decorative beads finish the band around the opening band to complete "Purple Passion Pocket Pouch Purse."

"Daisies! You've Come a Long Way, Baby"
Jan Ike Potter • Myrtle Creek, OR
Tie for third place

"This challenge was so much fun, combining lots of machine and hand work with 3-D embroidery flowers and leaves — I call it hours of flowers!" Jan Ike Potter said. The entire handbag, including the lining, is made of silk Dupioni. Pin tucking, quilting and bobbin work form the base of this anything-but-basic bag. Various dimensional flowers from Floral Dimensions 2 embroidery CD were stitched on organza and strategically placed on the bag and straps. A few ladybug charms complement the embroidery. The appropriate button with loop closure completes the bag, and inside is a matching coin purse with an embroidery daisy closure. "As always, naming a piece is as much a challenge as the project. I happened on the little brass ornament in a thrift store. Indeed, over the years, I've come a long way, baby," Jan said.

"Swimming with Turtles and Coral"
Donna Hixson and Colleen Hathaway
Bowling Green, KY • *Tie for third place*

The joint effort of two friends from different artistic backgrounds produced this underwater scene of hand-painted turtles swimming though hand-dyed fabric among coral and other sea life. One friend is the artist, and the other is the stitcher. The detail of the turtles was stitched free motion and appliquéd to the water background. Slub, eyelash and other fringed, fluffy yarns were couched to create the illusion of underwater plant life. Hand-stitched beads, buttons and rhinestones represent coral. A sparkle of blue rivets and metallic/rayon piping accents the finished edge around the opening of the bag. With the designs continuing around the bag and up into the strap, it's easy to understand why Donna Hixson and Colleen Hathaway named this handbag "Swimming with Turtles and Coral."

"Road Trip"
Terri Duhon • Shreveport, LA

Finding a map with color was Terri Duhon's design challenge for "Road Trip." She pieced maps from Mapquest.com to show the roads she travels in Louisiana, Arkansas and Tennessee to see family and friends. She printed the maps on Color Plus Fabrics and continued with her project. A decorative stitch in Sliver Thread follows the route from Shreveport to Lafayette, La., Rogers Ariz., and Memphis. Purple metallic rick rack separates and defines the sections and opening of the bag. To complete "Road Trip," Terri found motorcycle fabric to use as the lining! The image of Elvis, guitars and a "King of the Road" license on the lining makes this bag ready for a long ride.

"Flora with Butterfly"
Cindy Arriola • Tampa, FL

Cindy Arriola is an artist who enjoys sewing. She altered the handbag pattern to conform to her drawings on this faux suede and moleskin bag. Real suede and leather dimensional flowers in shades of wine and slate blue are attached to the bag with rivet centers. The cut edge of suede is a finished edge, curling to form 3-D effects. Hand-stitched stems and leaves made of embroidery thread connect the flowers together. Cindy cut the butterfly wings with a leather eyelet tool and accented the butterfly antenna with metallic thread. Silver metal rings dot the strap and complement the rivets. A magnetic snap with tab closure completes Cindy's "Flora with Butterfly."

"Paradise Pouch"
Nancy R. Jenkins • Lansing, MI

"I love novelty accessories and Hawaii. I thought the two were a perfect fit!" Nancy Jenkins said. Using velveteen, organza and cotton fabrics in vibrant colors as a foundation, Nancy created "Paradise Pouch" with a collection of Hawaii-themed computerized embroidery designs. She embellished the back and strap with a swimming fish and turtle, ocean wave, surfboard, bird of paradise, hibiscus, grass skirt, pair of sandals, palm tree and coconut drink. The patchwork is defined with a variety of decorative machine stitches, and the bag is framed with gold metallic piping and side panels of island print fabric. The Hawaiian scene, complete with guitar, lei and the word Aloha embroidered on the front, makes "Paradise Pouch" a perfect fit for a luau or tropical vacation.

"Purple Fantasy"
Marci Rohrer • San Francisco, CA

Anything goes when it comes to crazy quilting. Various combinations of threads, fabric and trims blend together to form a unique unit. No two are ever alike, and that's the beauty of crazy quilts. Silk Dupioni, cotton, lamé, brocade, satin and velveteen form the basic crazy quilt in a contrasting, but complementary color range. Marci Rohrer embellished the piecing with free-motion quilting using Candlelight thread and couching with eyelash yarns. A tassel braid accents one corner of the center panel. For added detail, purchased cording frames each section of the bag. A larger, fringed piping finishes the opening edge and completes Marci's "Purple Fantasy."

"Stepping Out"
Marci Rohrer • San Francisco, CA

Retro 50s girl is the focal point of Marci Rohrer's "Stepping Out." Using the stitch and flip method of piecing, Marci began with the center panel of her bag. The shape of the piecing outlines the dancing girl and continues to the edges of the panel. Random couching using Midnight Candlelight and eyelash yarn highlights the cotton fabric. The same couching detail extends into the strap of the bag. After trimming the bag with purchased cording, Marci added the final touch to the opening: large cording twisted with eyelash.

"Belize Valise"
Delnita Foust • Eureka Springs, AR

Inspired by photographs taken by her daughter and son-in-law during a recent excursion through Central America, Delnita Foust created "Belize Valise" out of hand-woven fabrics acquired on the trip. Using a Chico's Baja Bag as an example, she allowed the multi-textured fabric to become the basis for the bag. Turquoise and metallic beads hand-stitched to the center panel complement the textured fabric. "My precious grandmother taught me to sew when I was just a very young child, and it is the most priceless gift I have," Delnita said. The challenge came at a sad time in her life. "I had never entered a sewing challenge before, but this helped me concentrate on something hopeful and familiar — sewing."

"Good Times — A Joint Venture"
Laura Anderson and Susan Dye • Higginsville, MO

This project became a shared adventure for Susan Dye and her granddaughter, Laura. With some assistance, choosing the fabric, threads and beads was six-year-old Laura's job. She was in charge of the placement and design of the handbag components. But since Laura was a too young for Grandmother's big machine, the construction was shifted to Susan, who carried out Laura's plan. Heavy threads were couched in place. With the completion of the bag, "Good Times — A Joint Venture" by Laura Anderson and Susan Dye, became a reality.

"Polka Dot Pouch"
Jean Deister • Kenmore, WA

Beginning with a needlepoint kit from a craft store, Jean Deister designed the flap as the focus of "Polka Dot Pouch." To complement the flap, she hand-stitched silk ribbon embroidery flowers on the side panels to duplicate the needlepoint design. Polka dot fabric adds detail to corded piping on the edge of the strap, around the edges of the flap and between sections of the bag. Finally, Jean attached a magnetic snap to close the flap. With the right combination of machine and hand stitching, Jean created "Polka Dot Pouch."

"Dragonfly Crazy"
Bonnie Hargrove • Glen Carbon, IL

Originally designed to complete an ensemble for the American Sewing Guild Convention, Bonnie Hargrove's "Dragonfly Crazy" is a work of art in itself. Silk Dupioni crazy patch forms the base of her handbag, which is pieced and complemented with decorative machine stitches of embroidery thread. Double needle and couching add dimension. A 3-D organza dragonfly with a silk-ribbon embroidered body is the focal point of one side of the bag. Continuing with her design, Bonnie added computerized embroidery daisies from Cactus Punch Floral Dimensions. A ruffle at the opening edge constructed of bias plaid Dupioni and corded piping strip on the bias accentuates and frames the sections of the bag. Purchased beaded trim applied with hand-stitched seed beads finishes the edge. A "B" cleverly centered in the middle of an embroidered flower acts as a monogram or label for this vogue bag.

Linda's Gallery

Choosing the perfect handbag is challenging. Some women like to change their purses with every outfit, while others prefer to carry one handbag until it falls apart. Regardless of your preference, there can be one (or more than one!) perfect handbag for you.

Remember, the handbag is an extension of you — it is your constant companion, and it makes a fashion statement. You can draw attention with the bag you carry as well as the clothes you wear.

I like to make handbags because they are versatile and you don't have to worry about fitting a body. Each bag can have its own personality while also being an expression of my own.

All of these bags were made using the Perfect Bag Pattern. Each bag has its own unique history. Perhaps they will influence you to incorporate some of yourself in your bags.

Aren't old jeans a great canvas for creativity? They are ageless, and they capture the essence of fun, function and fashion. I decided to use my husband Jack's worn-out jeans and grandson Mike's outgrown jeans, to make a bag that would have frogs, bugs and other guy things. The patch pocket from Mike's jeans determined the pattern size to use. I left the pocket attached to the jeans and cut the center panel so the pocket was usable. I matched the original embroidery on one pocket with the double-corded piping to accent between the panels. An embroidery fusible appliqué given to me by a student was the perfect addition to the other pocket. Variegated jeans thread, decoratively machine stitched, tied the colors from the lining to the outside. A narrow strip of lining fabric covered the cut edges of the strap. For added texture, the side panels are cut at an angle. Both pairs of jeans had been washed and worn many times, so shrinking was not an issue. The worn edge of the pocket added character to this fun jeans bag.

I have had an affinity with frogs since the 70s. Lately, while experimenting on the Janome and using the arcing features, I inserted the letters f r o g five times. The arced letters formed an interesting snowflake-like design. Rather than stitch the designs randomly on the panel in the same position, I rotated each design several degrees to make the letters appear to be floating on the side of the bag. For variety, I used two different fonts. I also decided to try arcing backwards, so that the letters faced inward rather than outward. A twisted rayon thread gave the embroidery a herringbone look, and I added glitz with hot-fix crystals. The lining, a frog batik fabric, carried the theme throughout the bag, including the corded piping. On the other side of the bag, a slanted zipper made the pocket more accessible. The frog pull, a gift from a friend, was the perfect accent to finish the bag.

When a favorite T-shirt is too large or small, it's time to make a handbag! The textured design of the frogs was appealing, but the knit fabric was not suitable for the whole bag —so I interfaced the design area of the T-shirt with knit-type interfacing to make it more stable. With the knit stretching in one direction and the interfacing stretching in the other, the layers were bonded together. I used a home decoration fabric for most of the body and made the adjustable strap of webbing with D-rings and sliders. Corded piping of cotton quilting fabric accents the frogs, finishes the panels and coordinates with the lining. A decorative Riri zipper adds sophisticated style to this funky frog bag.

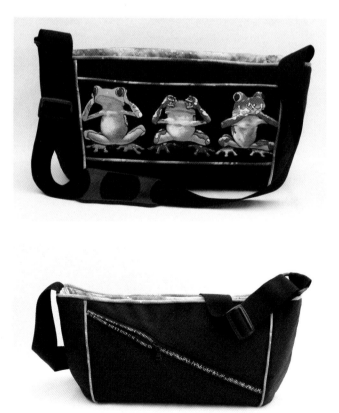

I began my sewing career at an early age, and I learned to save all the scraps — you never know when those small pieces will come in handy for another project. This wonderful textured bag evolved from the leftovers of an ensemble in the Fairfield Style Show. Colorful batiks from Hoffman Fabrics formed the spiral patchwork in the center panel. It was couched with heavier threads, cords and ribbons from YLI and Kreinik thread companies. The side panels are corded pintucks stitched with metallic thread in a double needle with a feather stitch and gimpe between the wrong side of the fabric and the bobbin thread. The seams and panels were separated with purchased metallic corded piping.

Since I didn't have enough fabric to make a strap, I used a chain.

This exquisite fimo clay pin caught my eye at one of the sewing and quilting shows, and I knew I just had to have it! I found these fabrics in my collection later, and I realized that I probably purchased them while thinking about the pin. Using some of my favorite techniques, I made the spiral patchwork, which formed the base for the pin. Crinkling (permanent wrinkles) and couching of heavier threads from Superior Threads formed the side panels with double-corded piping.

When Becky J showed me her Cross Stitch Tiger Eyes by machine and I discovered the Wild Things jungle prints by P & B Textiles, I knew that a bag was in the works. About the same time, I found the wonderful waxed cord and banana bark handles. It was the perfect combination. The focal point of the bag is the tiger's eyes peeking through the jungle. Zebra striped corded piping surrounds the cross-stitch design, and other fabrics finish the opening in one bag with corded piping, and the other with binding. The jungle theme follows into the lining as well. I stitched one bag with a wide opening and the other with a narrow opening. These bags are a tribute to the LSU tigers — or maybe it's just the wild animal in me!

I've been blessed with friends whose artistic abilities far surpass mine, and I love to incorporate their work into my handbags. Betty Cauthen, of Betty's Sunset Threads, was an artist whose touch made paint flow into beautiful designs. Her artwork included very special little people, both girls and boys. Another friend, Becky J. McNeill, developed Counted XS by Machine Embroidery. Becky programmed Betty's designs into cross stitch, and Linda created this clever bag, using Charms fabric from Benartex. The tiny plaid and paint-spotted fabric appropriately fits with the little stitching girl.

I have a weakness for buttons. I think everyone should have a button collection from which to draw — and sometimes the button can even be a focal point. I decided to use two made-for-each other buttons. Using variegated heavier cotton thread from YLI, I stitched straight lines, formed with a plaid design, which subtly enhanced the faux suede. A narrow strip of the suede was woven through the chain for a Chanel look. I added a personal touch with embroidery flowers from my CDs with Cactus Punch, Floral Dimensions and Floral Dimensions 2. Another button from my collection became the flower center.

For a classic look, add decorative stitching to basic black. I used a base of faux suede, with multiple lines of front-to-back straight stitching in the center panel. The stitching didn't need to be the same on both sides of the bag. The soft blue, red, green and purple variegated cotton quilting threads from YLI overlap in some areas, giving the illusion of ribbon. A double strap was appropriate for the wide opening.

Basic stitch-and-flip quick piecing makes a great project for beginners and advanced quilters alike. I began this project with embroidery arcing on batik fabric as the focal point, and I continued with contrasting batiks to complete the center panel. Black piping accents the various sections. Embroidery was stitched only on one side of the bag — notice how the look changes! This bag was nice with no design at all, but it comes alive with a large, blue embroidered flower from my Floral Dimensions CD pinned to the side.

It was a delight to find so many wonderful double-faced quilted fabrics recently. Fabri-Quilt produces many designs, including floral, Victorian, Oriental, geometric, western, country, seasonal and more. I just love the bright fabrics! By using a double-faced quilted fabric, the stitching time was reduced drastically. The edges were be finished on the serger. To make this project even faster, I purchased an undisciplined black-and-white striped fabric cut on the bias from ReadyBias. The fabric was already folded and cut to 1¼", the perfect width for binding. I used it for the corded piping accent, the binding on the pockets and opening, and finishing the strap. A large toggle button with loop functions closed the bag, and a slider and D-ring from Ghee's made an adjustable strap. When you need a tote, this is your bag.

This floral double-faced quilted bag was created from the end of the bolt of fabric. There was exactly ¼ yd. of fabric left. The strap and binding required ¼ yd. of companion fabric, and the purchased corded piping was left over from another project. There was just enough fabric left to make one inside pocket. Isn't it cute?

For this large bag, I needed extra fabric yardage layout to cut the strap on the lengthwise grain. This allowed for extra fabric to make a matching small bag. The braided strap with striped fabric on the cross-grain added a contrast to the binding trim. With a zipper pocket on one side and an open pocket on the other, this practical bag is easy to organize.

With a Scottish name like McGehee, I naturally incorporate plaids and tartans into my wardrobe. Matching plaids is a major obstacle for some stitchers, but don't let it keep you from using the bright fabrics. Cut one side panel out and place it on the fabric, right sides together, to cut the adjoining piece. It's that simple! Fussy cutting may require extra fabric. Be sure to double-check yardage before cutting. Using ¼" seam allowances makes it easier to match the plaids when stitching the seams together. Rather than attempting to match the center panel to the side panel, cut the center panel on point or bias. Sections of the bag are separated with antique gold cording. The same cording and bias plaid finish the opening. The strap actually was a drapery pullback originally! Other flowers from Floral Dimensions complement the plaid. What a nifty, attractive finish to an elegant bag!

Have fun making your handbags. Don't leave home without one!

about the author

Linda McGehee is known internationally for her extraordinary designs and innovative techniques. She has written award-winning books about the surface manipulation she has mastered. Her book "Creating Texture with Textiles," published by Krause Publications, showcases many of her projects featured in the prestigious Fairfield Fashion Show, Bernina Fashion Show, Statements, Capitol Imports and Better Homes and Gardens. Linda's second book with Krause, "Simply Sensational Bags," teaches the basics of bag construction and embellishment.

In addition to sewing handbags and creating texture, Linda has created 3-D designs for the embroidery machine through Cactus Punch. Floral Dimensions and Floral Dimensions 2 allow the sewer to create lovely dimensional flowers with various types of threads.

Linda has appeared on "Sewing with Nancy," "Sandra Betzina, "Kaye Wood's Quilting Friends," "America Sews with Sue Hausmann," "America Quilts," "Martha's Sewing Room" and QNN.

Traveling the globe to share her love of sewing, Linda teaches at sewing machine conventions, stores, guilds, and sewing, quilting and embroidery shows. She recently received the Excellence in Teaching Award at the American Sewing Expo. This award is unique because the attendees choose the winner.

Ghee's, her company, is the foremost supplier of handbag hardware and supplies in the US.

When not sewing and teaching, Linda enjoys the outdoors, cooking and photography with her husband, Jack.

resources

Baby Lock
www.babylock.com
Sergers and sewing machines for the love
of sewing.

Benartex
www.benartex.com
Leading supplier of creative 100% designer
cotton prints.

Becky J Designs
www.beckyjdesigns.com
Counted XS by Machine Embroidery.

Bernina
www.berninausa.com
Nothing sews like a Bernina.

Brother
www.brother.com
At your side — home appliance division.

Cactus Punch
www.cactuspunch.com
Embroidery digitizing: where perfection is the
common thread.

Coats & Clark
www.coatsandclark.com
Manufacturer of consumer sewing and quilting
threads.

Color Plus Fabrics
www.colorplusfabrics.com
All-natural fiber fabrics, paper-backed to feed
through any inkjet printer.

Elna
www.elnausa.com
Home sewing and embroidery machines.

Fabri-Quilt, Inc.
www.fabri-quilt.com
More fabric than you'll know what to do with,
but we're sure you can find a way.

Loralie Designs
www.loraliedesigns.com
Touching the heart with fun art — fabric
collections and machine embroidery.

Ghee's
www.ghees.com
Books, handbag patterns and embroidery designs by Linda McGehee; magnetic snaps, handbag hardware, zippers, and other accessories
for making handbags; fusible fleece and other
stabilizers for inside handbags.

Hoffman Fabrics
www.hoffmanfabrics.com
Designer and producer of superior quality
screen-printed, hand-painted and dyed cottons
and blends since 1924.

Husqvarna Viking
www.husqvarnaviking.com
Keeping the world sewing.

Janome
www.janome.com
Experience the memory craft — dream, inspire,
create.

Kreinik

www.kreinik.com
Here at Kreinik, we're all about thread.

Arova-Mettler

www.arova-mettler.com
The premium-quality sewing thread.

Oklahoma Embroidery Supply and Design

www.oesd.com
OESD provides the largest range of embroidery and sewing thread products available.

Olfa

www.olfa.com
Best-made cutting tools in the world.

P&B Textiles

www.pbtex.com
P&B Textiles is a leading supplier of 100% cotton fabrics for quilting and crafts.

Pfaff

www.pfaff.com
Feel the creative energy.

Pieces Be With You

www.piecesbewithyou.com
Groovin' Piping Trimming Tool.

ReadyQuilting.com

www.readybias-readytemplates.com
100% cotton ready-to-use continuous binding.

Riri

www.riri.com
Zippers — the brand of excellence.

Rowenta

www.rowentausa.com
Leading manufacturer of high-performance irons, steamers, steam generators and ironing boards.

Singer

www.singer.com
Sewing specialty.

Sulky

www.sulky.com
The premier decorative thread and stabilizer company.

Superior Threads

www.superiorthreads.com
Sew much more.

The Warm Company

www.warmcompany.com
Dedicated to providing innovative quality products for the quilting, crafting and sewing industry.

YLI

www.ylicorp.com
Unleash your imagination. Give free reign to your creativity with decorative threads from YLI.

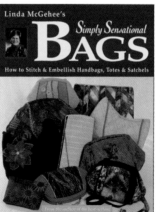